# THIS BOOK BELONGS TO

_____

_____

To Hana. – P.A.

To Lucas and Eli: may you soar high and cast a bright light. – O.C.

To all Asian American comic book artists who inspire us, specially Stan Sakai
and Jim Lee, whose art has been with me for a long time. – J.C.

immedium
Immedium, Inc.
P.O. Box 31846
San Francisco, CA 94131
www.immedium.com

First hardcover edition published 2020.

Edited by Lorraine Dong
Book design by Dorothy Mak

Printed in Malaysia
10 9 8 7 6 5 4 3 2 1

Library of Congress Cataloging-in-Publication Data

Names: Amara, Philip, author. | Chin, Oliver Clyde, 1969- author. | Calle,
  Juan, 1977- illustrator.
Title: Awesome Asian Americans : 20 stars who made America amazing / by
  Phil Amara & Oliver Chin ; illustrated by Juan Calle.
Description: First hardcover edition. | San Francisco, CA : Immedium, Inc.,
  2020. | Includes bibliographical references. | Audience: Ages 9-17 |
  Audience: Grades 4-6 | Summary: "This is an illustrated children's
  anthology of noteworthy Asian Americans: 20 groundbreaking men and women
  from diverse backgrounds and vocations" – Provided by publisher.
Identifiers: LCCN 2020011608 (print) | LCCN 2020011609 (ebook) | ISBN
  9781597021500 (hardback) | ISBN 9781597021555 (ebook)
Subjects: | LCSH: Asian Americans--Biography--Juvenile literature. |
  Celebrities--United States--Biography--Juvenile literature.
Classification: LCC E184.A75 A47 2020 (print) | LCC E184.A75  (ebook) |
  DDC 920.0092/95073--dc23
LC record available at https://lccn.loc.gov/2020011608
LC ebook record available at https://lccn.loc.gov/2020011609

ISBN: 978-1-59702-150-0

# AWESOME ASIAN AMERICANS

## 20 Stars Who Made America Amazing

By **Phil Amara**
and **Oliver Chin**

Illustrated by
**Juan Calle**

immedium
Immedium, Inc.
San Francisco, CA

# TABLE OF CONTENTS

# INTRODUCTION

In 2018, the phrase "Asian American" had its fiftieth anniversary. In 1968, students at the University of California (UC) at Berkeley coined the term when they founded the Asian American Political Alliance (AAPA). Fueled by the 1960s Civil Rights movement, AAPA protested for legal, political, and social equality for Asians in America as well. A year later, San Francisco State University (SFSU) and UC Berkeley, Davis, and Los Angeles (UCLA), founded the first college-level Asian American Studies programs in the United States.

Out was the label "Oriental." That term came from the Latin word "oriens" which meant rising. The sun rose from the "east." From Europe, the center of the Roman Empire and later the dominant colonizers of the world, Asia was east. Therefore to Europeans, anyone coming from the direction of Asia was "oriental."

America inherited this Eurocentric perspective and the definition of "Oriental": foreign, exotic, other. This racial profile stereotyped a stranger from somewhere else as an outsider who did not really belong "here." But what if people with Asian heritage wanted to control their own identities?

Asians have been Americans for centuries. In 2020, Asians were the fastest growing group of American immigrants. It is projected that "minorities" will become the majority of the US population by 2050.

However, since the global spread of a new coronavirus disease started in November 2019 (COVID-19), anti-Asian racism has spiked in the United States. By May 2020, the Center for Public Integrity reported that 30% of Americans witnessed someone blaming Asian people for the pandemic, and that 60% of Asian Americans had seen such behavior. At the same time, the *Washington Post* reported Asian American doctors and nurses have been increasingly harassed by bigots. This has been an unsettling reminder that prejudice is hard to eliminate.

Coincidentally, May is the month that Americans celebrate the cultures and contributions of Asians and Pacific Islanders. President George H.W. Bush had issued Presidential Proclamation 6130 on May 7, 1990 to officially recognize this annual commemoration.

Fittingly a new television documentary series *Asian Americans* debuted on PBS in May 2020. Co-produced by the Center of Asian American Media (CAAM), it told the histories of these communities for a new generation of citizens. CAAM Executive Director Stephen Gong said:

> These are American stories: stories of resilience in the face of racism, of overcoming challenges as refugees from war and strife, of making contributions in all sectors of society: business, technology, military service, and the arts. These Asian American experiences and voices provide a vital foundation for a future fast approaching, in which no single ethnic or racial group defines America, in which shared principles will define who we are as Americans.

Our book is presented in the same spirit. This collection profiles noteworthy people in chronological order. The families of these ten men and ten women came from different places to contribute to the United States and change it for the better. Asian Americans, Pacific Islanders, and Asians have enriched America's culture, economy, and creative spirit. Immigrants and their descendants continue to give of themselves to become part of the nation's essential fabric.

Not all are household names. Some have been almost lost to memory, excluded from public acknowledgement or history textbooks. Trailblazers lay the foundation to smooth the paths of those who follow. Their sacrifices deserve to be remembered. Their biographies can inspire readers to imagine ways to improve not only themselves but also society.

On every US coin and dollar bill is stamped another Latin phrase, "e pluribus unum." This slogan was used by the 1782 Continental Congress. Placed on the Great Seal, "out of many, one" describes how thirteen original colonies formed the United States. Today this motto applies to how every American can find strength by appreciating our fellow citizens' diverse backgrounds and accomplishments.

In this 21st century world, people seem to have an insatiable appetite for imaginary and idealized heroes, who wield marvelous powers and perform incredible feats. In actuality, many of our most effective and diligent champions have looked like us and labored in our very midst.

We look forward to learning about your amazing stories and adding them to the ones that follow.

# TYRUS WONG

### ARTIST

| | |
|---|---|
| Born: October 25, 1910 | Died: December 30, 2016 |
| Toisan, Guangdong, China | Sunland, California |

**"... [I]f you put down just what is necessary, you will have a great painting.
If you can do a painting with five strokes instead of ten you can make your painting sing."**

On a Southern California beach on the fourth Saturday of the month, a parade of animals would rise to the sky. Goldfish, dragonflies, owls, and pandas. Butterflies with eight-foot wingspans. A dance of nine snow cranes. A flock of 25 swallows. A 75-segment centipede, 145 feet long. The creator of more than two hundred kites was a spry elderly man. Tyrus Wong shaved Japanese bamboo, constructed the designs, and painted the kite fabric by hand. He preferred this hobby to a past one because "Fishing you're looking down. Kite flying, you're looking up." Plus, it reminded him of when he was seven years old and his father made him a kite.

"What Tyrus Wong brought to [Bambi's] art direction is just absolutely stunning. Thousands of small scale and large scale sketches were very lyrical and had that poetry that Walt wanted.

— Andreas Deja, animator,
The Little Mermaid, Beauty and the Beast, Aladdin

"I love to paint," Tyrus told Pamela Tom in her 2015 documentary *Tyrus* which aired on PBS' *American Masters*. "Anything else, I'm no good at all." Waiting decades for his due, Tyrus was lead artist on Disney's classic 1942 animated feature *Bambi*. Although not an animator, he took *Bambi* beyond conventional expectations and put his stamp on a whole generation's childhood. *Big Hero 6* designer Paul Felix said, "*Bambi* never goes away. We're constantly taking a look at it, to the point where we all know almost every single one of those sketches that Tyrus did… he's the one who set the template for the film's visual vocabulary."

Born in southern China, Wong Geng Yeo and his family were poor. Unable to afford ink or rice paper, his father instructed him to practice calligraphy with water on old newspapers. Seeking a better life, nine-year-old Geng Yeo and his father boarded the steamship *SS China* in 1920 to try their luck in America. The boy never saw his mother again.

No welcome waited on the other side of the Pacific Ocean. In 1882, the United States passed the Chinese Exclusion Act. The Wongs did what other Chinese immigrants did to survive: they pretended to be relatives of people already on the mainland.

The father assumed the name Look Get. The son became Look Tai Yow. Arriving at Angel Island Immigration Station off the coast of San Francisco, California, the child was separated from his parent. "It was like a prison," the boy remembered. With only one chance to pass the oral entrance interrogation, he memorized pages of answers about his fake family and passed. Now considered a "paper son," he reunited with his father. They moved to Sacramento and then Los Angeles. Teachers called him "Tyrus."

After enjoying a summer scholarship at the Otis Art Institute, fourteen-year-old Tyrus refused to return to junior high. His father borrowed money for the $90 tuition and Tyrus walked six miles roundtrip every day between Chinatown and school. Afterward, he earned annual scholarships, but used donated art supplies, and worked as a janitor and cafeteria busboy for his meals. Tyrus learned Western drawing techniques and admired the paintings from China's Song dynasty (960–1279).

After his father died, Tyrus graduated in 1935 and painted public commissions for the Works Progress Administration. Working as a waiter at the Chinatown restaurant Dragon's Den, he met Ruth Kim, a secretary for Los Angeles' first Chinese American immigration lawyer Y.C. Hong. They married in 1937 and soon had a daughter. Tyrus got a $22.50 / week job at Disney to make short Mickey Mouse animations. He was an in-betweener, an entry-level artist who filled in images between the main poses ("keyframes") drawn by veterans.

I didn't like doing in-betweening. All day you have to look into a lightbox and flip pages back and forth. It was difficult, and at the end of the day I thought my eyeballs were going to drop out.

Luckily, pre-production on *Bambi* had started. Tyrus read Felix Salten's book, then painted landscape samples for art director Tom Codrick. Walt Disney approved and Tyrus got the responsibility of setting the film's colors and mood. "I tried to keep the thing very, very simple and create the atmosphere, the feeling of the forest," he reflected. Although his art was done behind the scenes, it produced a poetic environment of mystery and emotion that all the other animators had to emulate.

Frank Thomas and Ollie Johnston, authors of the 1990 book *Walt Disney's Bambi,* wrote: "His paintings, styling sketches, watercolors, and pastels would give a whole new appearance to the picture, distinct from any we had previously given or would ever give any film."

However, as one of only two Asian artists, Tyrus faced some prejudice. When other artists went on strike, he continued to work. After the strike was over, he was fired in 1941. When *Bambi* debuted the next year, Tyrus was only listed in the credits as one of nine "background" artists.

Tyrus rebounded as a pre-production illustrator for Warner Bros. Studios for the next twenty-seven years. In a cinematic era before "previsualization" on computers, his conceptual illustrations enabled directors to decide how to film scenes and how the set could look. He contributed to the movies *Sands of Iwo Jima* (1949), *Rebel Without a Cause* (1955), *Around the World in Eighty Days* (1956), *The Music Man* (1962), *Camelot* (1967), *The Wild Bunch* (1969), and many others. Meanwhile, the Chinese Exclusion Act was repealed in 1943 and he became a US citizen in 1946.

Tyrus' imagination never stopped. At home he would go up to his *own* studio and work more. He collaborated with Ruth to sell his hand-painted silk scarves to boutiques. He decorated ceramic dinnerware that were sold in department stores nationwide. Playing records of Christmas carols (in June!) to help him imagine an elf or angel, he designed holiday cards, one of which sold more than one million copies.

His daughters Kim, Tai-Ling, and Kay remember their dad fondly. "He clearly knew he wanted to bring a Chinese brush feel to much of his work," said Tai-Ling. "It's possible he knew he had a unique style that was different from work done by others."

"By observing his surroundings, he could capture a feeling, solitude, peace, excitement, or joy," recounted Kim. "We'd often see him making small sketching movements with his drawing hand, transferring something he was looking at into a sketch in his mind."

Then at an age when other retirees planned their vacations, Tyrus started making kites. His daughters witnessed his inventive passion, "Our Dad was always creating art. Growing up, we benefited from his rich imagination and creativity — from his design of our family's home and garden to the handmade holiday gifts he created for us even when he was in his 90s."

Tyrus was invited back to work at Disney on its 1998 animated movie *Mulan*. He declined. Mouse life was behind him. However, in 2001, Disney inducted him into their "Legends" hall of fame. Walt's nephew Roy E. Disney said of Tyrus, "He only worked at the studio for three years and during that time, devoted himself to just one movie, *Bambi*. But what a film it was."

Tyrus' art exhibited in Los Angeles at the Chinese American Museum, Craft and Folk Art Museum, Academy of Motion Picture Arts and Sciences, and New York's Museum of Chinese in America. In 2005, the animation industry's Annie Awards recognized him for lifetime achievement.

In 2013, the Walt Disney Family Museum (San Francisco, California) honored him with a lifetime retrospective. It exhibited more than 265 of his pieces, along with a companion book *Water to Paper, Paint to Sky*. The gallery was within sight of Angel Island, where young Tyrus had been detained for three weeks. Tyrus told John Canemaker (in the 1996 book, *Before the Animation Begins*) that *Bambi* was "a minor, very small part" of his life. Tai-Ling also points out that as good as Wong was, his children did not think of their father's work as masterpieces, "I doubt if he saw them that way."

But generations of professional creators certainly have. "Tyrus was an inspiration, as an artist and a human being," said Pixar's *Up* and *Inside Out* director Pete Docter. "I met him when he was 99, and at that time he'd been retired for longer than I'd been alive.... He'd been so prolific and innovative in his artwork, in spite of the obstacles life threw at him. What an example to artists everywhere."

In 2016, Tyrus passed away at the age of 106. By then his legacy was appreciated. He expanded the artistic horizons of not just Disney films but all animated movies to come. He charmed a dream world onto a canvas, whether it was ink to paper or a kite in the wind, a creature soaring in the blue heaven above.

SOURCES

Canemaker, John. *Before the Animation Begins: The Art and Lives of Disney Inspirational Sketch Artists.* Hyperion, 1996.

Tom, Pamela, director. *Tyrus.* New Moon Pictures, 2015.

www.chsa.org/2013/11/water-to-paper-paint-to-sky-the-art-of-tyrus-wong-at-the-walt-disney-family-museum/

www.juxtapoz.com/news/tyrus-wong-water-to-paper-paint-to-sky-disney-family-museum-sf/

www.latimes.com/entertainment/arts/la-et-cm-tyrus-wong-kite-man-20161230-story.html

# Sono Osato

## DANCER

**Born:** August 29, 1919
Omaha, Nebraska

**Died:** December 26, 2018
New York, New York

*"Wherever I looked onstage, there were those with whom I had shared
so much – youth, energy, ambition. But above all there was the work, devotion
to the hard, precious work that aims always towards perfection."*

On December 28, 1944, Sono Osato readied to dance as Ivy Smith in New York Broadway's debut of the musical comedy *On the Town*. World War II raged in Europe. Fighting in the Pacific would continue until the United States dropped atomic bombs on Hiroshima and Nagasaki, Japan in August 1945. In the play, three US sailors had 24-hour shore leave in Manhattan to pursue romance. How would the audience react when a Navy man falls in love with Ivy, played by a Japanese American of mixed heritage?

Three years earlier, Sono performed ballet before and after the news of Japan's attack on Hawai'i's Pearl Harbor on December 7, 1941. Although it would take almost two months for the United States to strike back at sea, the government was ready to retaliate at home immediately. The next night in Chicago, the FBI arrested Sono's father Shoji as an "enemy alien." Quickly the United States forced more than 110,000 Japanese residents to abandon their homes and businesses, and imprisoned them. On December 14, 1945, anticipating a Supreme Court ruling the next day, the US War Department ended its three-year internment of Japanese Americans.

Born in Akita, Japan, Shoji Osato came to America at the age of nineteen. After surviving the 1906 San Francisco earthquake, he moved to Omaha, Nebraska. Working at a newspaper, he photographed Francis Fitzgerald in 1917, and they fell in love. However, Nebraska outlawed marriages between Asians and whites, so the two wed in the neighboring state of Iowa. Returning home, Francis was ostracized by her Irish-French Canadian family. Sono was born in 1919 and her sister Teru followed a year later. When visiting Shoji's family in Japan in 1923, the family survived the great Kanto earthquake.

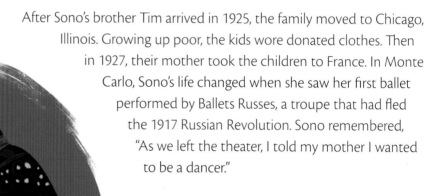

After Sono's brother Tim arrived in 1925, the family moved to Chicago, Illinois. Growing up poor, the kids wore donated clothes. Then in 1927, their mother took the children to France. In Monte Carlo, Sono's life changed when she saw her first ballet performed by Ballets Russes, a troupe that had fled the 1917 Russian Revolution. Sono remembered, "As we left the theater, I told my mother I wanted to be a dancer."

In 1929, the Great Depression forced the family to return to Chicago, where Sono enrolled in her first ballet class. In 1934, she auditioned for Colonel Wassily Grigorievitch de Basil who accepted her into Ballets Russes de Monte Carlo. At age fourteen, Sono was the first American, first Japanese, and youngest member ever. On her first day, she rehearsed *Swan Lake*. Luckily, the company spoke French, in which Sono was fluent.

While her parents became caretakers of Chicago's Japanese Tea Garden and Phoenix Pavilion, Sono traveled the world. She began a five-year relationship with Roman Jasinsky, a Polish dancer ten years her senior. No medical birth control existed when she became pregnant. Sono wanted to continue her career. Therefore her mother arranged for Sono to have an abortion, which was illegal at the time.

In 1940, the *New York Times* praised Sono's "exotic beauty" in her role as the Siren in George Balanchine's ballet *The Prodigal Son*. Famed artist Isamu Noguchi (who also was of mixed Japanese heritage) sculpted her likeness. She modeled fashions in the women's magazines *Harper's Bazaar* and *Vogue*.

But beneath the glamour, Sono knew her profession demanded grit:

> Unlike a musician, a dancer cannot trade in his instrument for another. Our bodies are all that we have, and we continue to move them beyond their natural limits, exposing them to perpetual hazards. If you want to dance, you learn to bear the pain.

In 1941, wanting a higher salary and more prominent roles, Sono joined New York's Ballet Theater (BT; now American Ballet Theater (ABT)). Then she met Moroccan-born architect Victor Elmaleh and fell in love "on the spot." However, his parents were Sephardic Jews who were against their union.

After Pearl Harbor, Sono's brother Tim enlisted in the US Army's 442nd Regimental Combat Team. At BT's request, Sono reluctantly agreed to use her mother's maiden name as her stage name. Nonetheless, the United States restricted Japanese from leaving America and denied Sono a passport for BT's tour of Mexico. Since California was now an "exclusion zone" where Japanese were no longer allowed, the government banned her from performing there too. Sono recalled,

> In shock, I asked myself, "What does this mean? I am an American." It had never occurred to me that the government would ever doubt my loyalty to my country, or deprive me of my work. This did both.

In 1943, Sono married Victor, who had been discharged from the Army, and professionally struck out on her own. Hired by choreographer Agnes de Mille as the "Premiere Dancer"

"...[A]NY STRONG ENDEAVOR THAT
GIVES YOU A SENSE OF JOY IS THE GREATEST
THING IN LIFE...." *-SONO OSATO*

in *One Touch of Venus*, Sono "stopped the show on opening night and has all but stolen it ever since," wrote New York's *PM*. The show swept the inaugural Donaldson Awards and she won Best Female Dancer.

Next, Sono joined *On the Town*, created by two 26-year-old Jewish American wunderkinds: composer Leonard Bernstein, and director and choreographer Jerome Robbins (the duo would reunite on *West Side Story*). It was one of the first Broadway productions to feature an integrated cast. The show included African American dancers and the first African American conductor.

Chinese American actress Anna May Wong may have been the last Asian American featured on Broadway back in 1931's *On the Spot*. Now Sono embodied the alluring Ivy Smith, winner of the monthly title of Miss Turnstiles (based on the New York transit system's beauty contest). Having performed for audiences the world over, as in 1938 in Berlin, Germany where Nazis attended, Sono knew how to focus and suppress her stage fright. She reflected:

> It was amazing to me that, at the height of a world war…
> a Broadway musical should feature, and have audiences
> unquestioningly accept, a half-Japanese as an All-American
> Girl. I could never have been accepted as Ivy Smith in films,
> or later, on television. Only the power of illusion created between performers
> and audiences across the footlights can transcend political preference,
> moral attitudes, and racial prejudice.

The dancer received rave reviews, caricatures by *New York Times* cartoonist Al Hirschfeld, and a feature in *Life* magazine. After numerous appeals, her father Shoji was granted parole to see her dance.

Sono wanted to start a family, especially after her sister Teru died from childbirth in 1946. Sono had two sons, Niko in 1947 and Antonio in 1950. In the 1947 film *The Kissing Bandit*, she acted as a Mexican love interest of crooner Frank Sinatra. Soon Sinatra would star in the 1949 movie version of *On the Town*. Featuring an all-white cast, it was a box office success and Academy Award winner.

Sono performed in a few more plays (including one written by a young Mel Brooks). But as she became more outspoken politically, her career suffered due to Hollywood's anti-communist "blacklist" in the 1950s. Her husband joined the New York office of his family's import-export business, founded World Wide Group in 1954 to distribute German cars (and some of the first Volkswagons), and then to develop billions of dollars in real estate. After the couple's passing, their Hamptons beachfront estate on Long Island, New York (a 7,200 square foot home on four acres) sold for $26 million in 2019.

In 1980, Sono wrote her autobiography, *Distant Dances*. Later, she endowed a scholarship at Career Transition for Dancers to help performers find new vocations after they stopped dancing. In the 2015 revival of *On the Town*, ABT's first African American principal dancer Misty Copeland reprised Sono's role.

Then on January 9, 2016, Chicago's Thodos Dance debuted its ballet *Sono's Journey* to commemorate the dancer's career. Sono attended the premiere. Artistic Director Melissa Thodos remarked:

> I wanted to tell Osato's inspirational story in the very medium she worked in. What fascinated me was the way her life and career had so many important parallels with our time. It's about diversity, and how this artist continued to grow and thrive while overcoming prejudice and professional limitations.

SOURCES

Oja, Carol J. *Bernstein Meets Broadway: Collaborative Art in a Time of War*. Oxford UP, 2014. Broadway Legacies.

http://blogs.wfmt.com/offmic/2016/01/08/sono-osato-96-reflects-on-dancing-with-the-ballet-russe-de-monte-carlo/

http://dancelines.com.au/chameleon-dancer-sono-osato-survived-racism-prejudice-broadway-star/

www.chicagoreader.com/chicago/sono-osato-japanese-american-ballet-dancer-prejudice/

www.neh.gov/humanities/2015/januaryfebruary/feature/the-original-miss-turnstiles

www.nytimes.com/2018/12/26/obituaries/sono-osato-dead.html

# Dr. Sammy Lee

## DIVER & DOCTOR

Born: August 1, 1920
Fresno, California

Died: December 2, 2016
Newport Beach, California

"[Prejudice] inspired me to perform. I was angered,
but I was going to prove that in America I could do anything."

It was August 5, 1948, and Sammy Lee was thirty-three feet high in the air . . . right where he wanted to be. From the surrounding stands, eyes gazed upward at him. His toes perched on the edge of a concrete cliff, he peered down at the Empire Pool below. Its glassy sheen sparkled in the light, but it was empty and waiting. After he jumped, Sammy had to enter its surface as straight as a railroad spike . . . at thirty miles per hour. If not, the water would hit him as hard as the concrete beneath his feet.

"THROUGH HIS MULTITUDE OF ACHIEVEMENTS AND AWARDS, [MY FATHER] TREASURED HIS FAMILY MOST. HE OFTEN STATED, 'THE MEDALS FADE BUT MY WIFE, DAUGHTER, SON, AND GRANDCHILDREN BECOME MORE GOLDEN AND PRECIOUS DURING THE LAST TWO-MINUTE DRILL OF MY GAME.'

— SAMMY LEE, JR.

It is not a natural impulse for a person to leap off a three-story building. However, Sammy had trained his whole life for this moment. This was his last "highboard" dive in the finals of the ten-meter platform event of the 1948 London Summer Olympics.

Earlier that week Sammy had won the diving bronze medal in the three-meter springboard and his teammate Bruce Harlan got the gold. But Sammy still had a promise to keep.

Sammy's parents were contractually obligated to marry each other, even before they were born. They immigrated from Korea, where they had lost two sons. In central California, they had two daughters. Once Samuel Rhee was born, his family moved south to open a grocery store. In 1932, Los Angeles hosted the Olympic Games. Seeing all the countries' colorful flags, Sammy recalled:

> Boy, I'll never forget the chill that just went up and down my spine. I said, "Gee, Papa, someday I'm gonna be an Olympic champ."
>
> He chuckled and said, "What in?"
>
> I said, "I don't know Papa, but I'll find it."

In junior high school, Sammy was hooked on diving with somersaults. He practiced at the Los Angeles Swim Stadium downtown at Exposition Park and also at Pasadena's Brookside Park pool. He remembered, "non-Whites could use the pool at Brookside only one day a week, on Wednesday." After "International Day" ended, the pool director pretended to drain and refill it for whites to use the next day.

At the age of fifteen, Sammy was hurt by racism again. A girl invited him to her party, but her parents made him leave because he was not white. Sammy recalled:

> So I went home and when Papa saw me crying in the backyard, he asked, "Why are you home so early?"
>
> I shouted, "Papa, why was I born a Korean and not white?"
>
> My father taught me a lesson I never forgot. He said, "Don't feel sorry for yourself. Feel lucky! You are born free to follow your dreams. You are an American, and if you are not proud of the color of your skin and your Korean heritage, then

how can your classmates respect you if you do not respect yourself? Show the world by being the best — the best you can be — and how proud you are of being an American of Korean ancestry!"

Soon Sammy won city championships. Inspired by a Korean marathoner who won gold at the 1936 Olympics in Berlin, Sammy practiced by jumping into a sand pit that he dug at his coach Jim Ryan's house. As a 5'2" junior, he was captain of the football team. Even though his high school's vice principal told him a non-white should not try to become student body president, Sammy ran and won. He was also named outstanding athlete and co-valedictorian of his class. But he could not attend even his own prom because the Pasadena Civic Auditorium would not admit "colored" people.

The 1940 and 1944 Olympics were cancelled due to World War II. At Occidental College, Sammy was the American Athletic Union (AAU) national champion in platform and three-meter springboard diving in 1942. His father told him, "You got to study as hard as you dive. And you got to become a doctor." Sammy replied, "I'll do that. I'll do both." In 1943, his father died and Sammy enrolled at University of Southern California's (USC) medical school. Decades later, Sammy said his greatest success was becoming a surgeon.

Sammy won the AAU platform again in 1946 as he joined the US Army to pay for his doctorate. In 1947, he graduated as a doctor, lieutenant, and Olympian headed to England.

At Wembly Stadium for his final dive in 1948, Sammy chose his favorite, the forward 3½ somersault. From the tower, he had have two seconds to rotate his body 3½ times in the air. He recalled the moment:

The whistle blows and there is dead silence and all you can hear is the trickle of the water from the ten-meter tower. Drip . . . drip. It sounds like a gong. And that time is just like when you think you're gonna die, your whole life goes by. Wow, I've waited sixteen years for this moment, and now it's here.

Sammy took a deep breath, soared through the air, and sliced through the water. One of the seven judges gave him a perfect score of 10. On August 5, he edged out Bruce Harlan and became the first Asian American man to win an Olympic gold medal. Earlier, Sammy had counseled his teammate Victoria Manalo Draves. On August 3, she became the first Asian American to win an Olympic gold medal, and on the 6th, she became the first American woman to sweep the springboard and platform diving events.

In 1950, Sammy married Rosalind Wong and they would have two children, Pamela and Sammy Jr. Then the Korean War began. Now a major in the US Army Medical Corps, Sammy asked his commanding officer whether he should train for the next Olympics. General Leonard Heaton replied, "Hey Sam, we have many physicians who can repair and treat the wounded, but we've only got one guy who can win the Olympic gold medal."

So, in 1952 in Helsinki, Finland, on his thirty-second birthday, Sammy became the first male diver to successfully defend his Olympic title, and the oldest to win a gold medal in diving. The following year he became the first Asian American to win the James E. Sullivan Award as USA's top amateur athlete.

With the AAU's 1953 James E. Sullivan Award.

In 1954, Sammy toured Asia as US cultural ambassador on a goodwill tour, where he met his father's friend, the first president of South Korea, Syngman Rhee. Major Sammy Lee departed from the Army in the following year. But he still was not allowed to buy a house in Orange County, California. The real estate agent explained, "I'm sorry, Doctor, but I have to eat, and I'd lose my job for selling to a non-white."

After President Dwight Eisenhower invited Sammy to the White House, the story got picked up by reporters such as Edward R. Morrow. In 1956, Sammy was praised by Groucho Marx on his hit TV show *You Bet Your Life*. Joining an outpouring of support, television host Ed Sullivan suggested, "You can buy the house right next door to me." Fortunately, Sammy had good neighbors. "When we moved to Southern California, we probably saw Sammy and his family every other weekend," said Draves' son David. "Sammy was a family friend for all my life."

Sammy became a prolific coach. Pupils included Pat McCormick (winner of four gold medals in 1952 and 1956) and Bob Webster (the second man to win back-to-back Olympic platform golds in 1960 and 1964). Sammy coached the US diving team in the 1960 Olympics, and the Japanese and Korean teams in 1964. In the 1970s, he tutored Greg Louganis who earned a silver medal on the tower in the 1976 Olympics and later won four golds. Sammy did not charge his athletes for coaching because "my coaches never charged me."

In 1968, Sammy was inducted into the International Swimming Hall of Fame. In 1984, he carried the torch and flag at the Olympics in Los Angeles. Six years afterward, he retired as an ophthalmologist and entered the US Olympic Hall of Fame. Sammy was an honored guest at London's 2012 Olympics and the next year his name graced a new USC diving tower and a Los Angeles public elementary school.

Sammy Lee died in 2016. His patients remembered him as a caring physician. Others remembered him as a giant in the world of sports. At Sammy's memorial, Webster reminisced:

> Some people come into our lives, leave a footprint on our souls, and we're never the same. Sammy was that person for me. He took a so-so high school diver under his wing and made an Olympic champion. He gave me the greatest gift and that was to believe in myself.

Louganis said, "At a time of intolerance, being Korean, he broke down racial barriers, setting an example of what it meant to be an Olympian."

SOURCES

"An Olympian's Oral History." Interview by Dr. Margaret Costa, 1999. LA84 Foundation. www.la84.org

*Sammy Lee Memorial.* www.youtube.com/watch?v=9gBZZVYNTWw

https://swimoregon.org/off-the-block-dr-sammy-lee-olympic-diver/

www.kcet.org/shows/lost-la/sammy-lee-a-life-that-shaped-the-currents-of-california-and-us-history

www.npr.org/sections/codeswitch/2016/12/05/504421352/sammy-lee-climbed-above-racism-dove-into-olympic-history

# Yuri Kochiyama

## ACTIVIST

Born: May 19, 1921
San Pedro, California

Died: June 1, 2014
Berkeley, California

"Knowledge of history can be used as a weapon to divide
us further or seek truth and learn from past errors and flagrant remisses.
Our ultimate objective in learning about anything is to try to create
and develop a more just society than we have seen."

On February 21, 1965, Yuri Kochiyama and her oldest son Billy joined the crowd entering the Audubon Ballroom in Washington Heights, New York City. Everyone had come to hear Malcolm X speak.

Three decades earlier, in 1931, the African American association Nation of Islam (NOI) was founded in Detroit, Michigan. Nearby in the city of Lansing, Malcolm Little was six years old. White supremacists had burned his family's house down two years before. Now they murdered his father who was a Baptist minister. As an adult, Malcolm joined NOI in 1956 and adopted the last name of "X" to reject his "slave" surname. Soon he became NOI's most outspoken member, challenging the Civil Rights movement led by Reverend Martin Luther King, Jr., who advocated integration through non-violent resistance. Instead, Malcolm X argued that blacks should defend themselves "by any means necessary."

In 1964, Malcolm X's growing stature threatened NOI's leader Elijah Muhammad who expelled him. Malcolm then visited Mecca, founded a new organization, and stated that African Americans' greatest enemy was racism and not whites. Yet, at the Audubon, he knew his life was in danger. His house in Queens had been firebombed a week earlier. On stage, he began to address his followers. Then chaos erupted. Three NOI assassins shot him. A photo published in *Life* magazine's March 5 issue showed Malcom X as he laid dying while Yuri Kochiyama gently cradled his head.

Yuri recalled later, "Malcolm X was the one person [who] changed my life more than anyone else, because he gave me a different perspective of the struggle in America." The path to her "political awakening" had not been easy. She tackled the difficult road ahead with a deep determination.

Immigrants from Japan, Yuri's parents settled in seaside San Pedro, California. Her father Seiichi Nakahara, who operated a fish market, and mother Tsuyako had a son Arthur in 1918. Mary Yuriko and her twin brother Peter followed in 1921.

Mary enjoyed her childhood. In high school, she became the first female to earn a varsity sports letter and be vice president. A local newspaper sports reporter and Presbyterian Sunday school teacher, she graduated in 1939 and attended Compton Junior College where she majored in Journalism.

But in 1941, Mary's world flipped upside down. On December 7, Japan's attack on Pearl Harbor incited the US government to imprison Japanese Americans. That very morning, Mary, a fresh college graduate, was home when agents from the Federal Bureau of Investigation (FBI) arrested her father, who had just returned from the hospital for diabetes treatment and ulcer surgery. He was detained six weeks and denied medical care. The FBI released him without charges and he died a day later.

Then the United States interned Mary's family. The Santa Anita racetrack was converted into an "assembly center" where they were forced to live in horse stalls. Next, they were transferred for two years to the swampland of Jerome, Arkansas. These traumas impacted Mary's life and her sympathy with African Americans enduring segregation. She recalled,

> In each instance there were senseless degradation, brutality, and hatred wrought by fear and ignorance caused by racism. So I remain passionately committed to doing whatever I can and saying whatever I must to eliminate racist assumptions and ideas.

In the concentration camp, Mary met her future husband Bill Kochiyama. A New Yorker, he had been interned in Topaz, Arizona. He volunteered for the US Army's 442nd Regimental Combat Team. Stationed in nearby Mississippi, he accompanied pals to Jerome to visit their relatives. After World War II ended, the couple married on February 9, 1946, and moved to Manhattan where they would have four sons and two daughters. Constantly hosting open houses and guests, their busy home was compared to Grand Central Station.

In 1960, the couple relocated uptown to Harlem, where Mary became active in the local community and Civil Rights movement. She joined the Harlem Parent Committee to demand more streetlights and better school education. She also joined the Congress of Racial Equality (CORE), an interracial group that organized the Freedom Rides to confront segregation in the American South.

Protesting for more minority construction jobs, Mary, her eldest son Billy, and others were arrested in Brooklyn, New York. On October 16, 1963, Malcolm X encouraged the group at their hearing in the courthouse. Overcoming her self-consciousness, Mary shook his hand and congratulated him for giving direction to his people.

Yuri and Bill.

Immediately, Mary wrote many letters to Malcolm X. Then on June 6, 1964, he visited the Kochiyamas' apartment to greet Japanese advocates of nuclear non-proliferation. Later, he sent her eleven postcards from nine countries as he traveled worldwide. After Malcolm X's death, Mary remembered her friend "was very much like the North Star, the most brilliant of all stars, which charts the course for all who follow." Dutifully she attended the annual pilgrimage to his gravesite until 1999, when she had a stroke and moved to California to be closer to her family.

As black factions became more revolutionary after Malcolm X's assassination, so did Mary. In 1968, she was one of the few non-blacks who joined the Republic of New Africa (RNA) that wanted to create a separate black nation in the southern United States. As an RNA "citizen," she discarded her western name "Mary."

Called "Sister Yuri" by fellow radicals, Yuri provided their support network. Her clearinghouse of information, phone numbers, and referrals was a database before personal computers and the Internet. But the FBI's counter intelligence program (COINTELPRO) targeted groups like the militant Black Panther Party as domestic threats and covertly campaigned to "expose, disrupt, misdirect, discredit, and otherwise neutralize" them. Soon dozens of Yuri's contacts nationwide were killed or behind bars.

For "political prisoners," people who were jailed for anti-establishment political beliefs, Yuri was the first person to call for help. At the intersection of the Black Power and Asian American movements, she organized demonstrations for black liberation and marches against the Vietnam War. She wrote thousands of letters at her kitchen table, which overflowed with so much paper that her family had no space to eat.

Yuri backed the independence of the territory of Puerto Rico, which chafed under both Spanish and American colonialism. In 1954, four Puerto Rican nationalists shot and injured five US congressmen. Demanding the Puerto Ricans' release from prison, Yuri participated with twenty-nine compatriots in 1977 to take over the Statue of Liberty for one day. Following the publicity over the protestors' arrests, President Jimmy Carter pardoned the remaining nationalist prisoners in 1979.

Meanwhile, the Kochiyamas galvanized Japanese Americans to petition the US government to redress their World War II internment and provide reparations for the injury caused. In 1981, Yuri was the keynote speaker at the first Day of Remembrance to commemorate

"SHE LIKED TO TALK ABOUT THE MOVEMENTS AND THE PEOPLE, BUT TO GET HER TO TALK ABOUT HER ROLE WAS ALWAYS VERY DIFFICULT, BECAUSE YURI IS SO OTHER-FOCUSED AND SO GENUINELY HUMBLE."

—DIANE FUJINO,
PROFESSOR OF
ASIAN AMERICAN STUDIES,
UC SANTA BARBARA

February 19, 1942, when President Franklin Roosevelt signed Executive Order 9066. Eventually in 1988, the US government passed the Civil Liberties Act, which offered a formal apology and $20,000 each to the surviving internees.

Enduring the deaths of her son Billy (1975), daughter Aichi (1989), and husband Bill (1993), Yuri persisted in speaking out at schools and wrote her memoir *Passing It On* in 2004. Fellow activist Angela Davis praised her compatriot who "fashioned an extraordinary life of commitment to peace, equality, and social justice. In this book, she passes on a legacy of humility and resolve, vitality and resistance, and, perhaps most important of all, hope for the future."

Though criticized for controversial, and sometimes contradictory, stances for praising foreign enemies, such as Mao Zedong and Ho Chi Minh, Yuri continued the struggle against oppression. The 2010 documentary *Mountains That Take Wing* recorded Yuri's conversations with Davis in 1996 and 2008, as they shared their common struggles to change a dominant status quo.

When Yuri died, Malcolm X's oldest daughter Attallah Shabazz commented:

> From the very moment I met Yuri Kochiyama in my childhood, it was apparent why she and my Father found such kinship with one another. They were "soul-siblings," sharing a spiritual and mission defined principle…. I was blessed to have grown up with her as an Aunt and example of human tenacity.

Yuri wrote, "The legacy I would like to leave is that people try to build bridges and not walls."

SOURCES

Fujino, Diane C. *Heartbeat of Struggle: The Revolutionary Life of Yuri Kochiyama*. U of Minnesota P, 2005. Critical American Studies.

Saunders, Patricia, and Rea Tajiri, directors. *Yuri Kochiyama*. Women Make Movies, 1994. Videorecording.

https://thesource.com/2014/06/04/the-source-remembers-yuri-kochiyama-activist-and-friend-of-malcolm-x/

www.discovernikkei.org/en/nikkeialbum/albums/472/

www.latimes.com/local/obituaries/la-me-yuri-kochiyama-20140604-story.html

# Daniel K. Inouye

## SOLDIER & STATESMAN

Born: September 7, 1924
Honolulu, Hawai'i

Died: December 17, 2012
Bethesda, Maryland

"So my fellow Americans, let us reject violence as a means of protest, and
let us reject those who preach violence. But let us not tempt those
who would hide the evil face of racism behind the mask of law and order."

In 1972, Republican Richard Nixon was re-elected as US President. Earlier that year, burglars were caught breaking into the Democratic National Committee's office at the Watergate Hotel in Washington, DC. Were the two events related? The Senate established the Select Committee on Presidential Campaign Activities to investigate. One of the committee's seven senators, Daniel Inouye, made his opening statement as public hearings were broadcast live on television nationwide in the summer of 1973:

At stake is the very integrity of the election process. Unless we can safeguard that process from broad manipulation, deception, and other illegal or unethical activities, one of the most precious rights — the right to vote — will be left without meaning. Democracy will have been subverted.

Protecting America was personal to Inouye. His grandparents emigrated to the territory of Hawai'i to labor on sugar plantations. Born in Honolulu, Inouye wanted to become a surgeon. He was a high school Red Cross volunteer in 1941, when Japan bombed nearby Pearl Harbor, which catapulted America into World War II. In its mania to contain "enemy aliens," the United States discharged Japanese Americans from the military and President Franklin Roosevelt authorized the internment of 110,000 Japanese on the mainland.

In 1943, to counter claims of racism, the US Army asked 4,000 Japanese Americans to volunteer. A pre-med freshman at the University of Hawai'i, Inouye enlisted. His father responded:

"[America] has been good to us. And now … it is you who must try to return the goodness of this country …. You are my first son and you are very precious to your mother and to me, but you must do what must be done. If it is necessary, you must be ready to . . . to . . . ." Unable to give voice to the dread words, his voice trailed off.

"I know, Papa, I understand."

"Do not bring dishonor on our name," he whispered urgently.

The 442nd Regimental Combat Team was a segregated group of Nisei (American born Japanese) with white officers. The 442nd's motto was "Go for Broke" and it became the most decorated unit of its size and length of service in American history. However, the price was high: its casualty rate was more than 90%. On April 21, 1945, Lieutenant Inouye led an attack near San Terenzo, Italy and destroyed three German machine gun nests with his Thompson submachine gun and hand grenades. He was wounded three times and his right arm was amputated without anesthesia. On May 9, the Nazis surrendered and the war in Europe was over.

Awarded the Bronze Star and Purple Heart medals, Captain Inouye recuperated for two years at the Percy Jones Army Hospital in Battle Creek, Michigan. Inouye befriended another seriously injured soldier, Bob Dole, who shared how he planned to go home to Kansas, run for office, and make it to Congress. Finally on his way home, Inouye traveled through Oakland, California. There, a barber refused to give him a haircut, claiming, "We don't cut Jap hair." Inouye recalled, "I was so tempted to strike him. But then I thought if I had done that, all the work that we had done would be for nil."

Back in Hawai'i, Inouye married Margaret Awamura in 1949. He graduated from college a year later. His dream of becoming a doctor was dashed, so he earned a law degree in 1952, and became a Democratic representative and then a senator in

With Bob Dole at Percy Jones Army Hospital.

the Territorial Congress. "The time had come for us to step forward," Inouye said of his fellow veterans who became politically active. "We had fought for that right with all the furious patriotism in our bodies and now we didn't want to go back to the plantation…. We wanted to take our full place in society."

In 1959, Hawai'i became America's fiftieth state and Inouye became the first Japanese American congressman and then senator in 1962. Two years later, he and his wife had a son Daniel Ken Junior. Dole remembered, "Shortly after taking office, he called me and said, 'Bob I'm here. Where are you?'" The Republican Dole entered the House of Representatives in 1960 and joined the Senate in 1968.

1n 1967, Inouye published his autobiography *Journey to Washington*. A year later in Chicago, he became the first person of color to give a keynote address at the Democratic National Convention. President Lyndon Johnson advised the Democratic presidential nominee, Vice President Hubert Humphrey (both of whom wrote forewords for Inouye's book) to pick Inouye as his running mate. Johnson thought Inouye's experience would counter mounting public criticism of the Democratic Party's handling of the Vietnam War, "He answers Vietnam with that empty sleeve. He answers your problems with Nixon with that empty sleeve." Humphrey demurred and lost the election.

In the 1973 Watergate hearings, Inouye became known for his cross-examinations of witnesses. The lawyer for Nixon's former domestic affairs adviser and Chief of Staff sneered, "What I mind is that little Jap." Colleagues and constituents rushed to Inouye's defense. The next day, Chairman Sam Ervin, Democratic Senator from North Carolina, declared:

I do not know a finer American. He showed his devotion to our country by fighting under its flag, not only for the liberty of our country, but for the liberty of the free world in the Second World War .... And he has proved himself in the latter days as one of the most dedicated Americans this country has ever known.

When reporters discovered that Nixon had authorized the burglary and tried to cover it up, Nixon resigned on August 8, 1974, rather than face impeachment.

Inouye chaired another Senate Select Committee in 1987, this time investigating the Iran-Contra scandal. President Ronald Reagan's administration illegally sold weapons to Iran to fund the Contras' guerilla rebellion against Nicaragua's communist government. The White House denied this and then tried to cover up its involvement, as participants withheld evidence and lied to Congress. Inouye stated,

Vigilance abroad does not require us to abandon our ideals or the rule of law at home. On the contrary, without our principles and without our ideals, we have little that is special or worthy to defend.

In 2000, President Bill Clinton awarded the Medal of Honor, the nation's highest military award, to Inouye and twenty-one other Asian Americans for their service in World War II. Clinton said, "Rarely has a nation been so well-served by a people it has so ill-treated."

In 2006, Inouye's wife Margaret died and two years later, he married Irene Hirano. In 2010, Inouye became the Senate's most senior member and president pro tempore, the highest-ranking Asian American politician in US history. President Barack Obama awarded the Congressional Gold Medal to him and other veterans of the 442nd.

Inouye died in 2012, ending a fifty-year career in the US Senate. Visiting Inouye's casket, which laid in state at the US Capitol Rotunda, Dole stood up from his wheelchair to salute his friend. Giving the eulogy at Inouye's funeral, President Obama recalled when he was eleven years old and watched the Watergate hearings:

Now, here I was, a young boy with a white mom, a black father, raised in Indonesia and Hawai'i. And I was beginning to sense how fitting into the world might not be as simple as it might seem. And so to see this man, this senator, this powerful, accomplished person who wasn't out of central casting when it came

The Washington Post

Nixon Denies Role in Cover-up
Admits Abuses by Subordinates

to what you'd think a senator might look like at the time, and the way he commanded the respect of an entire nation, I think it hinted to me what might be possible in my own life.

This was a man who as a teenager stepped up to serve his country even after his fellow Japanese Americans were declared enemy aliens; a man who believed in America even when its government didn't necessarily believe in him. That meant something to me. It gave me a powerful sense — one that I couldn't put into words — a powerful sense of hope.

A year later, President Obama posthumously awarded Inouye the Presidential Medal of Freedom.

Hawaiʻi would remember their most reliable congressional booster. Never losing an election, Inouye steered a steady supply of federal funding to the isles: "I'm not embarrassed or ashamed by what they call earmarks." Dutifully, Hawaiʻi renamed a highway, a solar telescope on Maui, and the Honolulu airport after him. In 2019, the US Navy followed suit, as his widow christened a new destroyer in honor of her husband, a stalwart defender of his country.

SOURCES

*Honolulu Star-Advertiser.* Inouye commemorative ed., 21 Dec. 2012.

http://cgm.smithsonianapa.org/stories/dan-inouye.html

https://obamawhitehouse.archives.gov

www.nps.gov/articles/inouyeww2.htm

www.nytimes.com/1973/08/02/archives/haldemans-lawyer-terms-inouye-that-little-jap.html

www.pbs.org/thewar/detail_5281.htm

www.senate.gov/artandhistory/history/common/investigations/Watergate.htm

# VICTORIA MANALO DRAVES

### DIVER

Born: December 31, 1924
San Francisco, California

Died: April 11, 2010
Palm Springs, California

*"You never know what a wonderful experience it is to concentrate on something, to set your goals and to work hard for them and then to eventually attain the ultimate ....The discipline that you learn for yourself, believing in yourself, and meeting other fine people ...."*

In 1948, countries were rebuilding from World War II and London hosted the Olympics. The first since 1936, these summer games did not invite Japan and Germany. But it was Victoria Manalo Draves' first international competition. Standing 5'1", this 23-year-old became the first American woman diver

"[Vicki] had a winning spirit, she had the skills, she had the consistency, and she was one heck of a competitor."

- Patricia McCormick, Four-Time Olympic Gold Medalist

to win gold medals in two events simultaneously. She was the first Asian American to win a medal (three-meter springboard), just two days before her friend Sammy Lee would win gold in ten-meter platform, and the first Filipino/a to win a gold medal.

However, these breakthroughs were not easily gained. People often judge others by their appearance, not their character. Vicki grew up facing discrimination and limited opportunities. Her father Teofilo Manalo was from Orion, Bataan, on the Philippines' largest island. Her English mother Gertrude Taylor came to San Francisco, California after her younger sister married a Filipino.

When Teofilo and Gertrude wed, California already had prohibited whites from marrying blacks or "Mongols" (Asians). Afterward, in 1932, the state legislature added "members of the Malay race" (Filipinos) as off limits. Gertrude worked as a maid. A cook and musician, Teofilo served an army colonel at the Presidio military base. The couple had a daughter Frances, a son Sonny who died as an infant, and then fraternal twin girls, Consuelo and Victoria.

As a child, Vicki wanted to learn ballet, but her family was poor. Overcoming her fear of the water, she started swimming when she was nine, paying a nickel to enter the Mission District's baths. Later she would take the trolley to the beach's saltwater Fleishhacker Pool (once America's largest pool), where a lifeguard told her about the posh Fairmont Hotel on Nob Hill. The hotel's Swimming and Diving Club hosted the waterworld greats of the time, like national diving champion Helen Crlenkovich, coached by Phil Patterson.

"I didn't start diving until I was sixteen," reflected Vicki. She wanted to improve and inquired at the Fairmont about practicing. However, Patterson told Gertrude her daughter could swim only if Vicki hid her Filipino roots and used her mother's maiden name, Taylor. In hindsight, Vicki concluded: "Instead of including me in the club, which everyone else belonged to, he formed a 'special' club just for me — the Patterson School of Swimming and Diving. I think he was a prejudiced man. It wasn't special for me. It was his way of separating me from the others."

Vicki then trained at North Beach's Crystal Bath Plunge, under the guidance of Charlie Sava and Jimmy McHugh. She graduated from high school but withdrew from San Francisco State Junior College when World War II began. Embarking on the amateur diving circuit in 1944, Vicki left her hometown for the first time. In Shakamak State Park, Indiana, she won third place in an AAU contest.

Then Vicki commuted across the bay to Oakland's Athens Athletic Club to train under Lyle Draves. He coached Zoe Ann Olsen who became the youngest three-meter springboard national champion, and would win a record thirteen AAU springboard diving titles. The Iowa native taught Vicki platform diving. In the oral history *Tales of Gold*, Vicki recalled:

> All this time, I had been diving on just sheer guts and whatever natural ability I had. Nobody had explained to me how to walk on the board, where to place my arms, how to lift up into a dive and the reasons behind all this. Lyle started me over completely, making me begin with very simple dives. I just wish I had had his coaching from the beginning. I think I would have been a far different diver.

Working as a secretary for the Army Port Surgeon's office, Vicki met fellow diver Sammy Lee. They would swim at the oceanfront Sutro baths (once the world's largest indoor swimming facility). In the meantime, she recounted, "I was not aware that [Lyle] had entered me in some competitions, but I was not able to dive because of racial prejudice." For example, after the war ended, the Fairmont Hotel admitted Lyle's other athletes to its meet but would not allow Vicki to enter.

After Teofilo's death, Vicki joined Lyle in Southern California. They married in 1946 and Sammy gave Vicki away at the wedding. Immediately, Lyle guided Vicki to three straight national championships on platform and the 1948 springboard title. Next, she contended at the Olympic trials in Detroit, Michigan. There she won the platform and came in second on springboard (Olson took first and Patty Eisener third). Soon she set sail with the Olympic team while Lyle paid his own passage to meet her in England.

Vicki and Lyle.

In London, Vicki insisted that the Olympics announcer introduce her as "Victoria Manalo Draves." At Wembley Stadium's indoor pool, contestants had eight dives on the springboard. On August 3, before her last attempt, she trailed Olsen in the standings. Shaking nervously, she confided her fear of failure to Sammy, who gave her a pep talk. Then she nailed her back 1½ layout. The American women swept the three-meter competition (Olson silver, Eisener bronze). Three days later, after six dives from the platform, Vicki won that contest too (Eisener earned silver). Afterward, Vicki enjoyed a dinner with her mother's siblings.

*Life* magazine named Vicki a top 1948 US Olympian, along with seventeen-year-old Bob Mathias, the gold medal decathlete. Calling her the "Olympics' prettiest champion," *Life* gushed, "Had there been a beauty contest at last year's Olympic Games, the raven-haired girl shown here would have won it…."

Turning professional, Vicki toured the United States and Europe in aquacades (water shows) with Lyle and other famous swimmers such as Buster Crabbe (two-time Olympic medalist; 1936 *Flash Gordon* actor), Johnny Weissmuller (five-time Olympic gold medalist; 1932 *Tarzan* actor), and Esther Williams (three-time AAU swimming champion; actress). Hollywood came calling, too, but Vicki turned down stereotypical film roles as a pretty South Seas native.

A highlight of her travels was diving for the Philippines President Elpidio Querino at the Malacañang Palace. Vicki recognized how sports had opened doors for her:

> Fortunately, through my diving, I was able to meet all my relatives on both my mom's and dad's side. In 1949, I was invited to the Philippines, and I spent a wonderful month there. I was not from a family of means, but fortunately athletic clubs sponsored me, and that gave me a chance. I just can't express how much diving did for me.

Later, the couple settled down in Southern California and taught their four sons (David, Jeffery, Dale, and Kim) the sport. Their aquatics program trained Pat McCormick, Paula Jean Myers, and Sue Gossick, who helped the US diving team medal at every Olympics from 1948 to 1972. In 1969, Vicki was inducted into the International Swimming Hall of Fame.

In October of 2006, San Francisco named a two-acre park after Vicki. "I thought after all these years they would have forgotten about me," Vicki said. "I am so overwhelmed that my accomplishments from so long ago are still remembered."

Vicki once played as a child in the park, known then as Columbia Square. It held sad memories for local Filipinos. In 1521, explorer Ferdinand Magellan claimed the Philippines as a colony for Spain. To end the Spanish American War in 1898, Spain sold the Philippines to the United States for $20 million. But Filipinos continued their fight for independence. The 1899 Philippine American War caused more than 200,000 Filipino deaths in three years and the US Army displayed spoils from looted churches at the square.

Since then, Filipinos have become the largest Asian ethnic population in California, and the second largest in America. As park supporters battled with developers to defend the plot, nearby Bessie Carmichael Elementary school (named after Vicki's elementary school principal) was rebuilt. It provided San Francisco's only Filipino bilingual program and enrolled the highest percentage of Filipino students in the city.

Long retired, an older Vicki recounted her love of diving, "That's when you feel like you're flying." Even though she felt the sting of racism, she still had a "patriotic feeling, doing something for your country" when she competed.

This real life aquawoman is a model for anyone fighting upstream. Her park plaque aptly states that Vicki Manalo Draves was "an inspiration for all athletes." In practice, she dove one hundred times a day. Her name left little to chance. Manalo means triumph in the Filipino dialect Tagalog, and Victoria is the Roman Goddess of Victory.

SOURCES
"An Olympian's Oral History." Interview by Dr. Margaret Costa, 1999. LA84 Foundation. www.la84.org
Victoria Manalo Draves Interview. www.youtube.com/watch?v=iMOtX_UCcRs
www.nytimes.com/2010/04/30/sports/olympics/30draves.html
www.sfgate.com/bayarea/article/SOUTH-OF-MARKET-City-to-name-park-after-1948-2631043.php
www.sfgate.com/sports/article/VICKI-DRAVES-Pioneer-Olympian-made-quite-a-2868925.php

# Bruce Lee

Martial Artist & Actor

Born: November 27, 1940
San Francisco, California

Died: July 20, 1973
Kowloon, Hong Kong

*"True mastery transcends any particular art. It stems from mastery of oneself —
the ability, developed through self-discipline, to be calm, fully aware, and completely in tune
with oneself and the surroundings. Then, and only then, can a person know himself."*

A 1973 movie *The Game of Death* presaged video games: 5'7" Billy Lo, clad in a yellow tracksuit, fights his way up a pagoda to steal a treasure. But to reach this prize, he must defeat bosses of increasing difficulty. The "5th Floor Guardian" is the 7'2" giant "Mantis," played by the 1971 Most Valuable Player (MVP) in the National Basketball Association (NBA), Kareem Abdul-Jabbar.

"In every industry, in every profession, ideas are what America is looking for. Ideas have made America what she is, and one good idea will make a man what he wants to be."

—Bruce Lee

"The Chinaman (who emerges impressively enough to justify a series of his own) lends a deft touch of exotica with advice on how to 'learn the art of dying.'"

Then Bruce auditioned for the Eurasian lead in the ABC television series *Kung Fu*. But producers disliked his accent. Instead, they hired the white actor David Carradine to speak stilted English. Simultaneously, Bruce created his own martial arts Western where he would be the hero, *Ah Sahm, Warrior*. He shelved it when his 1971 Hong Kong movie *The Big Boss* became a surprise hit.

Big screen success snowballed. In Golden Harvest's 1972 *Fist of Fury*, Bruce defeated dozens with whirling nunchakus. Then he made *The Way of the Dragon* where he bested karate king Chuck Norris. In December of that year, Ip Man died in Hong Kong and, seven months later, his finest pupil would perish nearby under mysterious circumstances during a heat wave.

With *Enter the Dragon* in 1973, Bruce became the most popular Asian American actor in the world. Battering enemies, including future stars Jackie Chan and Sammo Hung, bare-chested Lee became iconic in death. *The Hollywood Reporter* wrote, "Bruce Lee's last movie is the only one that gives him the star treatment he deserved. His charismatic presence is remarkable in *Enter the Dragon*, and it's a shame he didn't have the chance to become the great, unique star he seemed destined to be."

Bruce's fame inspired imitators and profiteers, who reworked his unfinished *The Game of Death* with stunt doubles and released it in 1979. Brandon tried to follow his father's footsteps. In 1993, he starred as a resurrected avenger in *The Crow*. However, he was accidentally shot on the set by a loaded prop gun and died. Brandon was buried next to his father's grave in Seattle. Then a month later came the movie *Dragon: The Bruce Lee Story*, based on a book written by his mother Linda. In 1994, *The Crow*'s theatrical success magnified the family's tragic curse.

Bruce became the muscular model for action heroes to come. He was memorialized in toys, t-shirts, statues, songs, and video games. His detailed notebooks that recorded his practices and philosophies were mined by book publishers.

In 1999, *Time* magazine named Bruce as one of 20th century's most influential people. In 2004, the Library of Congress preserved *Enter the Dragon* in the National Film Registry, and in 2014, Seattle's Wing Luke Museum started exhibiting his archives. Meanwhile, Shannon started the Bruce Lee Foundation but wrestled with his Hong Kong family over his legacy. In 2008, she produced a television series about Bruce's life. She started a *Bruce Lee* podcast in 2016, and two years later acquired his licensing rights back from Universal Studios. Cinemax aired Shannon's television production *Warrior* in 2019, which was based on Bruce's treatment written nearly fifty years before.

Bruce said, "Always be yourself, express yourself, have faith in yourself." He did not like to swim, was not good at driving, and did not have great eyesight. To those who exploit his image, his defenders rise. Kareem, the NBA Hall of Fame's leading scorer, and six-time MVP and champion, wrote in 2019:

> First rule of Bruce's fight club was don't fight — unless there is no other option. He felt no need to prove himself. He knew who he was and that the real fight wasn't on the mat, it was on the screen in creating opportunities for Asians to be seen as more than grinning stereotypes.

SOURCES
https://blackbeltmag.com/arts/chinese-arts/yip-man-wing-chun-legend-and-bruce-lees-formal-teacher
www.brucelee.com
www.historylink.org/File/3999
www.hollywoodreporter.com/news/kareem-abdul-jabbar-bruce-lee-was-my-friend-tarantinos-movie-disrespects-him-1232544
www.washingtonpost.com/news/retropolis/wp/2018/07/31/the-new-yellow-peril-how-u-s-film-critics-reviewed-bruce-lee-movies-in-his-day/

# Dr. Flossie Wong-Staal

## BIOLOGIST & VIROLOGIST

Born: August 27, 1947     Guangzhou, Guangdong, China

*"For me, as for most researchers, the main motivation is simply the satisfaction of making discoveries, finding out things that no one knew before."*

Thought to have come from chimpanzees in the early 20th century, the human immunodeficiency virus (HIV) spreads through bodily fluids. It weakens people's immune systems so they get sick from other infections. Late stage HIV is lethal and is called acquired immunodeficiency syndrome (AIDS). HIV and AIDS spread across the globe in the 1970s and still have no cure. In 2019, AIDS was the primary cause of human death due to infectious disease, and the fourth leading cause of death worldwide.

"ONCE YOU IDENTIFY THE GENES, THEN YOU CAN TRY TO FIND WAYS TO INHIBIT THEM, ESPECIALLY IF THEY ARE CRITICAL FOR THE VIRUS."

— FLOSSIE WONG-STAAL

Thirty-eight million people have HIV and almost as many have died from AIDS-related diseases since the epidemic started. However, the rates of infections and mortality have gradually declined. That is due in part to the scientific contributions of Flossie Wong-Staal.

In 1947, Flossie was born Wong Yee Ching, the third of four children, in Guangzhou, China. For his import-export business, her father traveled south to the nearby British colony of Hong Kong. When the Communists overthrew the Nationalist government in 1949 and millions of Chinese fled, Flossie's father stayed in Hong Kong. In 1952, the rest of the family finally managed to join him.

In Hong Kong, Flossie attended a Catholic school taught by American nuns. She remembered, "Since I did not want to be another Mary or Theresa, I asked my father to choose something unusual. He saw a list of names for typhoons that hit Southeast Asia, and picked 'Flossie.'" In high school, students were encouraged to focus on science, so Flossie did likewise. Following friends to America, she enrolled at UCLA. In 1968, she became the first child in her family to graduate from college, earning a *magna cum laude* degree in Bacteriology, which is the study of microscopic living organisms.

Continuing her studies at UCLA, she married Steven Staal in 1971. The next year she earned a doctorate in Molecular Biology (the study of life-giving properties of molecules, such as proteins and genetic material) and was awarded "Woman Graduate of the Year."

In 1972, the couple had a daughter Stephanie and Flossie's husband got a job with the National Institutes of Health (NIH), the United States government agency that researched biomedical and public health, based in Bethesda, Maryland. She got her own assignment there in 1973.

Flossie joined Robert Gallo's lab, which investigated oncogenes. Oncogenes are mutated genes in tumor cells. When oncogenes are activated, normal cells (the smallest basic unit of life) are converted into cancer cells, which divide uncontrollably and can lead to the death of the larger organism. Gallo's team also studied retroviruses, a type of virus that hijacks host cells to replicate itself.

A retrovirus' genetic code is in the form of ribonucleic acid (RNA). The retrovirus uses an enzyme called "reverse transcriptase" to command the infected cell to copy the virus' RNA into deoxyribonucleic acid (DNA). The virus' DNA then is inserted into the infected cell's DNA, and the host cell becomes a factory to make copies of the retrovirus. Flossie recalled:

At the time, there was no indication that such viruses existed in humans. Most of the hard-core scientists didn't believe in human retroviruses and called them "human rumor viruses." It wasn't a pleasant atmosphere at the time, but we persisted and Robert Gallo was the first to isolate the human retrovirus, human T cell leukemia virus (HTLV), in the late 1970s. That broke the ground.

In 1978, Flossie was a senior investigator in the laboratory of tumor cell biology at NIH's National Cancer Institute (NCI). In 1982, she became section chief of molecular genetics of hematopoietic cells that can develop into all types of blood cells. By then, the AIDS epidemic was spreading exponentially around the world. Governments increased funding for research. The competition and pressure to understand the disease grew.

The year 1983 was a breakthrough for Flossie. She not only had another daughter Caroline but also made the discovery of a lifetime. Her and Gallo's team identified HIV as the cause of AIDS, independently but simultaneously with a French research team led by Luc Montagnier. Flossie recounted:

> We were again in the minority, and most people at the time were looking at all kinds of wild potential causes of AIDS. But we stuck with our hypothesis that a retrovirus was involved and went down the path looking for evidence of retroviruses. In 1983, our lab at NIH first isolated viruses from AIDS patients. My group was brought on board once the virus was propagated in tissue culture and we recognized it as a new virus. My job was to understand what this virus was. So we were the first to clone and sequence the virus. We also showed the diversity of HIV — the reason why it is so difficult to make a vaccine or avoid drug-resistance issues.

HIV attacks immune system cells, evades detection, and mutates (changes its genetic code) constantly so that vaccines and drugs are not effective on newer and different forms of the virus. She summarized:

> We need to understand what the virus is at the molecular level. And as it turns out, the virus was very complicated, so we had to identify each gene. There are a number of novel genes not found in other retroviruses. We have to not only show that they ... exist, but what they do.

In 1985, in the midst of a divorce, Flossie mapped HIV genes. This key development led later to the creation of a blood test that could tell if a person was HIV positive.

Flossie became chair of AIDS research in 1990 at UC San Diego (UCSD). That year the Institute of Scientific Information reported that her papers were the most cited of any female scientist in the 1980s. NIH set up centers for AIDS research and in 1994, Flossie was named director of the UC system center. The same year she co-founded the biotech company Immusol and was elected a member to the Institute of Medicine for the National Academy of Sciences.

In 2002, Flossie left UCSD to become Immusol's Chief Science Officer for genomics. The same year *Discover* magazine named her one of the "50 Most Important Women in Science." In 2007, Immunsol hired a new CEO, Jeff McKelvy, who later married Flossie. She was inducted into the National Women's Hall of Fame in 2019 along with ten others that included US Supreme Court Justice Sonia Sotomayor and actress Jane Fonda.

HIV patients now can benefit from anti-retroviral therapy (ART), which can block the virus from entering the cell and replicating. This keeps the level of HIV in one's body low, reduces the risk of transmission, and allows the immune system to stay strong. However, the race for a cure continues.

As someone who is trilingual (Mandarin, Cantonese, and English) with more than forty-five scientific patents to her name, Flossie recognized the benefits of working together across borders for a common cause:

> These days, to be successful in science, you have to be able to articulate your ideas and promote them, so that people are interested in collaboration and invite you to future meetings. That's how you build your reputation. The days of being a lone scientist working in your lab are gone.

While the pursuit for an AIDS vaccine continues, humanity faces a new threat from another virus, COVID-19. In 2020, the coronavirus quickly spread worldwide. However, many countries did not coordinate their responses or act immediately to contain the pandemic. By July 2020, COVID-19 had infected more than ten million people worldwide and had killed more than 500,000. In the United States alone, more than 125,000 people died, greater than the combined number of American soldiers who died in combat since the Korean War.

Again, scientists must collaborate to research, experiment, and find effective treatments and hopefully, one day, a cure.

SOURCES

"Dr. Flossie Wong-Staal." Oral History, National Institutes of Health, 1997.

*Genomics & Proteomics*, Mar. 2003, p. 22. www.geopromag.com

http://shethoughtit.ilcml.com/biography/flossie-wong-staal/

https://info.umkc.edu/unews/celebrating-women-in-stem-dr-flossie-wong-staal/

https://orbitalelements.wordpress.com/2014/05/28/stem-female-role-model-spotlight-flossie-wong-staal/

www.unaids.org/en/resources/fact-sheet

# Dr. Steven Chu

## PHYSICIST & TEACHER

Born: February 28, 1948      St. Louis, Missouri

*"As the saying goes, the Stone Age did not end because we ran out of stones; we transitioned to better solutions. The same opportunity lies before us with energy efficiency and clean energy."*

Science, technology, engineering, and math (STEM) solve real-world problems. If anyone embodies STEM, it is Steven Chu. However, in his scholarly family, Steven may be the only "underachieving" Nobel Prize winner ever. "I could manage only a single advanced degree," he confessed. "I was to become the academic black sheep." Modest about his accomplishments (280 scientific papers, 18 patents, and 32 honorary degrees), Steven has nourished his mind like few have.

During World War II, Steven's parents left China and met as graduate students at the Massachusetts Institute of Technology (MIT). His father Ju Chin Chu became a professor in Chemical Engineering and his mother Ching Chen Li studied Economics. When the Communists took over China, the couple stayed in America and had three sons: Gilbert (1946), Steven (1948), and Morgan (1950). Growing up in Garden City on Long Island, New York, Steven recalled, "I loved building things with my hands," tinkering with toy rockets, models, and Erector sets. In high school, his physics and math teachers inspired him. Steven reflected:

> ...working with your hands and building things gives you a spatial intuition that turned out to be invaluable once I became a scientist. I could see things in my head very clearly and rotate them around. This idea of picturing things geometrically has always been a part of my thinking. The layperson doesn't think of that in terms of physicists; they think in terms of mathematical equations. I only discovered later that most physicists do that.

Steven studied Math and Physics at the University of Rochester, New York. After graduating in 1970, he got his Physics PhD from UC Berkeley in 1976. There, Professor Eugene Commins mentored him in experimental physics. Steven reminisced, "He had one remarkable quality that I wish I could copy, and that is, he made all of his students feel special, and that they could do something."

Steven admired both Albert Einstein and New York Yankee Yogi Berra. The famed physicist inspired Steven's studies and the Hall of Fame baseball catcher provided amusing wisdom such as "you can observe a lot by watching." In 1978, Steven moved to AT&T's Bell Laboratories in New Jersey. In 1980, he married Lisa Thielbar and they had sons Geoffrey (1981) and Michael (1984).

At Bell, a colleague Arthur Ashkin shared his dream: "Wouldn't it be nice if you can hold on to an atom with light?" Working late and watching a blizzard outside, Steven had a eureka moment: "What if you cooled down the atom first? Don't hold onto it, but maybe in the process of cooling it down, it's going to hang around for enough time that you can have a chance of grabbing onto it."

Steven's lab results sound like science fiction, but here goes. At the atomic level, the laws of quantum mechanics apply. Steven tuned a laser to the wavelength that an atom

(moving towards the laser) could absorb. He explained, "The light that the atom absorbs exerts a scattering force that slows the atom down." He fired three pairs of lasers at a sodium atom to cool it to almost absolute zero (-459.67 Fahrenheit), slowing it from 2,500 mph at room temperature to one mph. Stuck in "optical molasses" and caught by a seventh laser's electromagnetic force, it fell into a trap which was the size of a grain of sand.

"Laser cooling" enabled advancements in atomic, molecular, and optical (AMO) physics, ultra-precise atomic clocks, and "ultracold" chemistry such as freezing water... with a laser!

Steven's time at Bell Labs was "magical" but he got the itch to instruct. "I wanted to leave behind something more than scientific articles. I wanted to teach and give birth to my own set of scientific children," he said. "I began teaching with the idea of giving back; I received more than I gave." In 1987, Steven went to Stanford University and soon chaired the Physics Department. He applied his laser technique to biology to create "optical tweezers" to handle molecules like DNA. In 1997, he shared his physics Nobel with two others who independently developed "methods to cool and trap atoms with laser light." Divorced in 1995, Steven now married physicist Jean Fetter. Then he shaped Bio-X, Stanford's biomedical program and its new $150 million center.

In 2004, Steven headed the Department of Energy's Lawrence Berkeley National Lab (LBNL). He directed 3,400 employees and a $430 million budget to focus on climate and energy research. Five years later, President Barack Obama asked him to lead the Department of Energy (DOE), which President Jimmy Carter had established in 1977 as the twelfth cabinet department. Steven was the first scientist and Nobel laureate to be a cabinet secretary and the first Asian American to be DOE Secretary. Managing 100,000 employees and a $27 billion budget, he oversaw energy security and policy, from prices and supplies to conservation and environmental protection (such as cleaning up nuclear weapons).

Immediately, Steven promoted Advanced Research Projects Agency–Energy (ARPA-E) to support technologies that had high potential benefits. This program was like the Defense Department's Defense Advanced Research Projects Agency (DARPA), which funded the development of the Internet and self-driving cars. Steven connected mankind's historically unchecked energy consumption to global warming. "The climate problem is the unintended consequence of our success," he said. Since man-made global warming threatened life on earth, it was "time to help steer America and the world towards a path of sustainable energy."

Nevertheless, Steven still had to deal with the messy business of fossil fuels. In 2010, British Petroleum's (BP) Deepwater Horizon offshore rig exploded in the Gulf of Mexico and leaked 60,000 barrels of oil per day. The *New York Times* reported that Steven took "a commanding role": he suggested that gamma rays could see where the oil valve failed and sketched a fix on a napkin. Obama recalled, "It looked like a little hat. There were some numbers next to it." The White House sent it to BP whose engineers literally made a tighter cap to plug the leak.

Science can be political. Politics can be scientific. "You have to keep your wits about you, you have to dispassionately analyze what's the best path to go forward," Steven said. "Breakthroughs will happen, setbacks will happen. You use those breakthroughs to work around those setbacks to go forward."

Scientific methods (recognizing a problem, collecting facts, and testing potential answers) can fail in politics when adversaries devalue science. Steven found this out the hard way when the DOE had an additional $35 billion to fund clean energy projects. One loan went to Tesla Motors who paid it back. Another went to a company that made solar panels but it went bankrupt. Politicians, who supported the fossil fuel industry, seized on its failure to combat aid for "green" energy.

In 2019, the International Monetary Fund (IMF) reported that fossil fuels accounted for 85% of all global subsidies in 2015. If the fossil fuel industry paid its true costs, that "would have lowered global carbon emissions by 28% and fossil fuel air pollution deaths by 46%, and increased government revenue by 3.8% of GDP [Gross Domestic Product]." IMF calculated that in 2015, the United States actually spent $649 billion on subsidies (including higher consumer prices and environmental damage). This was more than its military spending and almost ten times its education spending. It was thirty times more than its budgeted fossil fuel subsidies (which itself almost equaled the DOE budget).

Steven became the longest serving DOE Secretary. In 2013, he returned to Stanford and intensified his commitment to renewable energy. The world is quickly switching to alternative sources like wind and solar, leaving "dirty" methods like coal behind. The United States is playing catch up.

On the health of the environment, Berra, a fellow Missourian, may have put it best: "The future ain't what it used to be." But Steven predicts that changes must come because we are in a "climate emergency" and "time is running out." In 2019, he became president of the American Association for the Advancement of Science (AAAS). Reducing air pollution and increasing battery storage require STEM innovations. Steven said:

> I'm very positive about science and the role it plays for the benefit of humankind. If one looks historically over the past 400 years, all the way up to today, many benefits have come from unfettered, uninstructed, curiosity-driven research that has led to unexpected but huge benefits to society.

SOURCES

http://globetrotter.berkeley.edu/people4/Chu/chu-con1.html

https://alumni.berkeley.edu/california-magazine/spring-2011-articles-faith/high-energy-physicist

https://newrepublic.com/article/100037/steven-chu-energy-obama-solyndra

www.nobelprize.org/prizes/physics/1997/chu/facts/

www.vice.com/en_us/article/jpp4w4/forget-solyndra-steven-chu

# Shahid Khan

## ENGINEER & CEO

Born: July 18, 1950        Lahore, Punjab, Pakistan

*"I think players, and every human being, has a right to speak what their opinion is. There's no issue as far as that goes, whether it's NFL or anybody else. We are American citizens, we have a social, civic responsibility to be active in causes we believe in."*

He has been called the personification of the American Dream. What is Shahid Khan's secret? The billionaire Pakistani American owns the National Football League's (NFL) Jacksonville Jaguars and English soccer's Fulham Football Club. Prodded by his son Tony, in 2019, he invested in television entertainment's All Elite Wrestling, featuring grapplers Cody Rhodes, John Moxley, and Kenny Omega. Shahid's deep pockets make it a legitimate rival to World Wrestling Entertainment (WWE), the big dog in the yard.

This billionaire balances a fan's enthusiasm with a businessman's savvy. "I love it. In the NFL, you win or you lose, and the money still shows up," he said. Shahid's handlebar mustache makes his face one of the most recognizable in sports. But he was not born with a silver spoon in his mouth.

Shahid hails from Lahore, Pakistan. This is where the Purna Swaraj (1929 Declaration of the Independence of India from British rule) and the Lahore Resolution (1940 demand that India's Muslims get a separate homeland of Pakistan) were written. In 1947, Britain granted the region's independence only when Pakistan was partitioned from India. Lahore became the capital of Pakistan's Punjab province and the second biggest city after Pakistan's capital Karachi.

Rafiq, Shahid's father, was a lawyer who sold surveying equipment. The mother Zakia was a math professor. On hot summer nights, Shahid and his two sisters and brother slept outside. As a child, he built radios to sell and rented his comic books to friends. Shahid and his dad watched cricket matches when the stadium opened to free admission after tea time.

In 1967, Shahid's parents gave their sixteen-year-old son a one-way ticket and $500 to study at the University of Illinois at Urbana-Champaign. When he got to America, his dorm had not opened. His shoes ruined by the snow, Shahid slept at a YMCA for $2/night. The next day he got a job washing dishes for $1.20/hour. According to Shahid, this wasn't peanuts... it was gold:

> That was more than 99% of the people back home [had] in Pakistan. I realized right then that this was the land of opportunity and I could control my own fate. Less than 24 hours after arriving, I had already discovered the American Dream.

Shahid joined the college fraternity Beta Theta Pi as its first non-white member. He recalled his undergraduate days:

> I had to overcome a lot of barriers. Until 1947, it was illegal for people from the subcontinent to migrate to the US. The subcontinentals were the last ethnic minority to gain citizenship. You assimilate. My name was too hard. They said, "Shad is what we are calling you." You go with the flow.

Shahid studied Industrial Engineering, watched football, and met his future wife Ann Carlson. After graduating in 1971, he joined Flex-N-Gate, which made after-market bumpers for autos. Making bumpers was inefficient: welded from more than a dozen pieces, they were heavy yet weak. Promoted to chief engineer, he saw the potential to sell directly to car manufacturers themselves.

With $13,000 in savings and a $50,000 Small Business Administration loan, Shahid founded Bumper Works in 1978. His innovative bumper was stamped from one sheet of steel; this reduced the vehicle's weight and improved its fuel economy.

But Flex-N-Gate sued Shahid for infringement and he defended himself in court. Flex-N-Gate's revenues were $17 million but it was losing money. In 1980, Shahid bought his former employer for $800,000. The following year he married Ann, and in 1982, they had a son Tony and later a daughter Shanna.

Shahid hustled to keep his company running. America's biggest automaker General Motors liked his bumper but told its larger suppliers to copy the design. So he went to Japan and convinced Isuzu, Mazda, and Toyota to install his bumpers on their cars destined for America. In the 1980s, as Japanese auto imports rose, the US auto industry lost jobs and many of Shahid's Rust Belt competitors went out of business.

Flex-N-Gate expanded its product line. Eventually its bumpers would sit on most cars sold in America. In 2019, *Forbes* magazine ranked it as one of the fifty largest US private companies with more than 24,000 employees, 65 plants, and $8 billion in revenue. *Forbes* named Shahid as one of the 100 richest people on earth (and wealthiest Pakistani). Like many NFL owners, he owns a yacht as long as a football field: the $200 million *Kismet* boasts a basketball court, pool, spa, helipad, and a weekly rental price of $1.2 million.

"Racism, in all its forms, will kill. It kills people, it kills communities, it kills dreams, it kills hope. For many Americans, now is the moment. Never has that been clearer. I don't want to waste this moment."

—Shahid Khan, June 3, 2020

Shahid became an American citizen in 1991, but his path to success has had potholes. After 9 / 11, he suffered racial profiling when US immigration detained him upon returning from Canada to Detroit on a business trip. In 2009, the Internal Revenue Service dinged him for dubious tax shelters. After a decade researching the NFL, in 2010, Shahid bid for 60% of the St. Louis Rams for $750 million. However, Stan Kroenke, the 40% minority owner, matched the offer and won. Shahid wasted two years negotiating. "You have to take your lumps and face reality," he rationalized. "There's always some good in something bad happening to you, and you look for that."

Then Shahid targeted Jacksonville: the Jaguars were one of the NFL's least successful, popular, and valuable teams. In 2012, he borrowed $300+ million to buy the franchise for $770 million. Unfortunately, after hearing the news, enough Floridians cast racist slurs against him that the seller Wayne Weaver gave his buyer a chance to back out. That episode made Shahid even "more determined" to be the NFL's first non-white owner.

Of Flex-N-Gate's sales, 90% came from North America. Shahid wanted to grow his auto and sports businesses globally. In 2013, he purchased Britain's venerable Fulham FC for $200+ million. Following the playbook of international expansion, he immediately tried to boost Jacksonville's popularity: now the Jags would play one game each season in London.

Winning games has not been Shahid's only challenge. A Republican, he voted for Donald Trump for president and donated $1 million to his inauguration. In January 2017, Trump ordered a travel ban for visitors from seven mostly Muslim nations. Shahid admitted this was "kind of a sobering time for somebody like me." He said, "The bedrock of this country [is] immigration and really a great separation between church and state" and that it would be bad to close the door to "the tens of thousands of people who can contribute to the making of America."

Then in September 2017, controversy erupted when San Francisco 49er quarterback Colin Kaepernick kneeled during the national anthem to protest police violence against African Americans. After Trump cursed him, on September 24, Shahid locked arms with the Jaguars in London's Wembley Stadium to support free speech. This was the first time an NFL owner publically stood with his players on the issue. Shahid wrote, "It was a privilege to stand on the sidelines" after Trump's "divisive and contentious remarks." He continued, "That's why it was important for us, and personally for me, to show the world that even if we may differ at times, we can and should be united in the effort to become better as a people and a nation."

Racing ahead is Shahid's main gear. He was Urbana-Champaign's 2013 commencement speaker after donating $10+ million. In 2016, he bought Toronto's Four Seasons Hotel for $171 million, the most expensive Canadian hotel sale ever. In Florida, he renovated the Jags' football stadium and won Jacksonville's 2017 contract to develop the nearby Shipyards area. He became majority owner of the Black News Channel, which launched as a cable television network in 2019.

Nicknamed by British tabloids as "the 'tache with the cash," Shahid offered to buy Wembley for $788 million in 2018. Some British complained about a foreigner controlling their iconic landmark. Shahid withdrew his bid but planned to add a second Jaguar game at the arena starting in 2020.

Shahid's teams have not become champions, but in 2019, *Forbes* ranked the Jacksonville Jaguars 23rd out of 32 NFL franchises, with a value of $2.3 billion. "If you aren't learning, you are regressing, because more growth comes from failure than from success," said Shahid.

The 2020 pandemic caused a drastic decline in travel as well as in car buying and production. As professional sports leagues faced uncertain schedules and attendance, the NFL cancelled its 2020 international games. On this rocky road, it will help to have good bumpers.

SOURCES

"Face of the Franchise." *60 Minutes*. 28 Oct. 2012.

www.fool.com/investing/general/2015/06/02/flex-n-gate-whos-behind-this-american-dream-story.aspx

www.forbes.com/sites/briansolomon/2012/09/05/shahid-khan-the-new-face-of-the-nfl-and-the-american-dream

www.jacksonville.com/article/20111203/NEWS/801240122

www.washingtonpost.com/news/sports/wp/2017/09/24/shahid-khan-the-jaguars-owner-who-stood-with-his-team-has-long-espoused-the-american-dream/

# HELEN ZIA

## AUTHOR & ACTIVIST

Born: 1952         Newark, New Jersey

**"We have to speak up. Nothing gets done unless you speak up, whether it's in America or anywhere else."**

On June 19, 1982, Vincent Chin, a 27-year-old Chinese American, celebrated his upcoming marriage. A draftsman at an engineering firm and a waiter, he had his bachelor's party in Highland Park, a city within Detroit, Michigan. The US auto industry had collapsed and many blamed it on competition from Japan — and anyone who looked Japanese. At an adult bar, Ronald Ebens, a Chrysler plant superintendent, and his 23-year-old stepson Michael Nitz, singled out Vincent and were overheard using racial epithets. The two groups were thrown out of the club. The two white men grabbed a baseball bat from their car and attacked Vincent in a nearby McDonald's parking lot. Nitz held Vincent's arms as Ebens swung the bat repeatedly at Vincent's head. Four days later, Vincent was removed from life support. His wedding guests went to his funeral instead.

Nitz and Ebens never spent a day in jail. Nine months later, after pleading guilty to manslaughter, the pair was sentenced to three years probation and fined $3,000 by a judge who did not call witnesses or have a prosecutor present at sentencing.

A laid-off Chrysler autoworker herself, Helen Zia followed the local news. Frustrated by the injustice, she recognized the racism she suffered as a child. She was a long way from home, trying to find her calling. This became the turning point that directed her life.

Helen grew up with five siblings in New Jersey where few Asians lived. Her mother, Beilin Woo, was a young widow when she met and married Yee Chen Zia in New York City's Chinatown. A translator with General Chiang Kai-shek's staff in Nationalist China, Yee found that his skills were not marketable in America. He created a small home business: the family made baby trinkets that he peddled to flower shops. He enjoyed writing literature in Chinese and English. So proud of his heritage, Yee sued Encyclopedia Britannica, Inc. for errors in its China entry.

Growing up when many saw Asian Americans as foreigners, Helen felt out of place, not fully Chinese or American. "I definitely grew up hearing every kind of taunt, and it would make me angry," she told Bill Moyers in his PBS TV series *Becoming American: The Chinese Experience*. "You never knew when somebody would yell at you, 'Go back where you came from.'"

Although her father insisted that "the proper place for an unmarried Chinese daughter is to stay at home with her parents," Helen received a full scholarship to attend nearby Princeton University. There she encountered the rising Asian American movement. "I learned that I was an Asian American," she recounted. "I learned that I didn't have to call myself Oriental, like a rug. It was like a light bulb going off." She co-founded the Asian American Students Association and obtained a grant to visit China in 1972. She graduated in Princeton's first coeducational class in 1973.

Next, Helen attended Tufts University School of Medicine in Boston, Massachusetts. Living in the South End, she actively organized her Black, Latino, and Asian communities. Quitting med school after two years, she recalled, "I finally mustered the courage to ruin my parents' dream — and that of nearly every Asian immigrant parent — to have an offspring who is a doctor, who will care for them in their old age."

Instead, in 1975 Helen became a construction worker in her neighborhood. She helped found the Boston Women's Union. That prompted her fellow activists of color to accuse her of being gay, which they asserted was a "white disease." Though Helen was privately questioning her own sexual orientation, she had not come out yet. When they asked if she was a lesbian, she replied, "No, I'm not." But she would answer differently in the decades to come.

In 1976, Helen drove out to the Midwest "to learn what it meant to be an American in America's heartland." After two years as an autoworker, she was laid off with millions of other manufacturing workers. She became a journalist for Detroit alternative weekly and monthly magazines, covering the travails of a city whose Asian American population was less than 1%.

Spurred into action by Vincent Chin's death, Helen did community organizing to galvanize public awareness, form alliances, and strategize on how to hold Vincent's killers accountable. She co-founded the American Citizens for Justice, which spurred the first US criminal civil rights case that involved an Asian person. Helen was interviewed in the 1987 documentary film, *Who Killed Vincent Chin?* (nominated for an Academy Award). She found her voice to advocate for a pan-Asian American movement to combat discrimination.

Climbing the editorial ladder as an investigative journalist, Helen moved back to the East Coast and eventually became editor-in-chief of a travel magazine. In 1989, she was the executive editor of *Ms.* magazine and worked with noted feminists Robin Morgan and Gloria Steinem. She wrote award-winning articles about date rape, the global system of garment sweatshops, and women who join white supremacist groups.

Befriending Lia Shigemura, Helen relocated to San Francisco, California in 1992 for a new job and the pair became domestic partners the following year. She co-edited the educational reference book *Notable Asian Americans* and in 2000, her first book *Asian American Dreams: The Emergence of an American People* was published.

Weaving in her own family's journey, Helen detailed key moments for Asians in American history, most never mentioned in school textbooks. In one chapter, she writes about her own coming out of the closet and the fight for marriage equality in the Asian American community.

The following year, Dr. Wen Ho Lee wrote his memoir, *My Country vs. Me*, together with Helen. A Taiwanese American, Dr. Lee was a nuclear weapons scientist for twenty years at Los Alamos, New Mexico. In 1999, the US government falsely accused him of spying for China, imprisoned him in solitary confinement for nine months, and then released him with an apology.

Helen married Lia in 2004 and again in June 2008 in San Francisco, as one of the first same-sex couples to legally marry in California. That year she carried the Olympic torch in San Francisco before the Beijing Olympics. In 2010, Helen became a witness in the federal trial for marriage equality that reached the Supreme Court, which legalized same-sex marriage throughout the United States.

In 2007, Helen was designated a Fulbright Scholar to research her 2019 book *Last Boat Out of Shanghai: The Epic Story of the Chinese Who Fled Mao's Revolution*. After World War II,

the Communists defeated the Nationalists in China, spurring the exodus of millions. Helen tracked the chaotic escapes of four people, including her mother who was adopted. In her investigation, she learned her parents legally arrived in the United States, but their visas ran out as they stayed on as refugees. They could have been deported, even after Helen was born. But because her parents had American-born children, the court granted them permanent residency with "green cards." At that time, the Immigration and Naturalization Service (INS) decided that separating parents from their children would have been "an extreme hardship and unusual cruelty."

As the executor of Vincent Chin's estate, Helen remembered his mother Lily who returned to China with a broken heart and died a few weeks before the twentieth anniversary of her adopted son's death. "She died feeling that if she hadn't adopted him, he'd be alive," Helen mused sadly. Through that grueling struggle came hard-won safeguards for others.

After some claimed that civil rights was only about black and white, Helen argued, "Vincent's case established that every immigrant, whether Latin, Asian, Black, white — every American was clearly protected by federal civil rights law." She further noted, "[h]ate crime protection laws now include perceived gender and disability. Victim impact statements also became more accepted after the Vincent Chin case."

Nevertheless, the fight continues to stand up for immigrants, refugees, victims of government mistreatment, women, and the poor. Helen commented:

> … an injustice to one is an injustice to all. No one is truly equal and free until everyone is equal and free. When a society allows anyone to be treated as less than equal and therefore less than fully human, we not only rob those people of their full humanity, we also become complicit in their mistreatmen…. Our lives and rights as human beings are inextricably linked, there are no degrees of separation.

SOURCES

Choy, Christine, and Renee Tajima-Peña, directors. *Who Killed Vincent Chin?* Film News Now Foundation, 1987.

https://china-underground.com/2018/08/22/interview-with-helen-zia/

www.helenzia.com

www.pbs.org/becomingamerican/

www.womensmediacenter.com/profile/helen-zia

# DOLLY GEE

## FEDERAL JUDGE

Born: 1959                     Los Angeles, California

*"Oftentimes we limit ourselves, and it is important sometimes to get out of your comfort zone and to accept the possibility that you might be able to do something in another field that you might not have necessarily thought about for yourself."*

After her father died in a civil war, fifteen-year-old Jenny Flores fled El Salvador to join her aunt in America. The INS arrested her at the US-Mexico border. Jenny was strip searched, imprisoned with men and women near Los Angeles, and denied education, recreation, and visitations. In 1985, a class-action lawsuit was filed against the United States for mistreating migrant children like her. In 1997, the United States consented to the Flores Settlement Agreement (FSA) to provide a standard quality of care for detained undocumented minors and to ensure their rapid release from detention to adult relatives or licensed shelters.

When Jenny was detained, Dolly Gee had just become a lawyer a few miles away and knew nothing about Jenny's case. Soon, Dolly would devote her legal career to protecting workers, fighting against discrimination, bridging the divides between groups, and eventually upholding the rights of society's most powerless.

The Gee clan in China's Guangdong province traces its roots to Zhu Xi, an influential Confucian scholar during the Song dynasty. Despite the family's scholarly roots, later generations turned to farming in southern China's rural hinterlands due to economic hardship, warfare, and migration.

In 1848, gold was discovered in California and news spread worldwide via merchant ships. In China, America became known as "Gold Mountain." The Gold Rush ended but the Golden State still attracted migrants to toil on farms and in garment factories for lives better than those they left behind. Dolly's great-great-grandfather joined thousands who departed Toisan in southern China to come to America. He worked on the Transcontinental Railroad that was completed in 1869.

Gradually, whites, who feared Chinese competition for jobs, stoked anti-Chinese sentiment. This resulted in discrimination, massacres, and the first US immigration law that banned an entire group of people based on ethnicity and nationality. The 1882 Chinese Exclusion Act prohibited the immigration of Chinese laborers and denied citizenship to people born in China. Unable to stay, Dolly's forefather returned to China. Her parents grew up in Toisan's small farming villages that had no running water or electricity.

In the 1930s, Dolly's grandfather left China for Brooklyn, New York. In 1941, his fifteen-year-old son, Jimwah, joined him. To learn English, "Jim" attended kindergarten. He also worked for his father, who had established a small shop making soy sauce and pickled cabbage.

During World War II, Jim joined the US Navy and served as a gunner's mate on the *USS Myrmidon, LST-948*, a repair ship that serviced the Pacific fleet, such as at Iwo Jima. After the war ended, he married his wife Helen and they moved to southwestern Los Angeles. There they had a son Kelvin and Dolly Maizie Gee arrived seven years later.

Jim became an aerospace engineer at Rockwell International and later worked on NASA (National Aeronautics and Space Administration) projects ranging from the Apollo space missions to the Space Shuttle program. Helen, who had been a schoolteacher in China, spoke little English and worked as a seamstress in a sweatshop. Dolly recalled, "She didn't teach me how to sew because her hope was that I would never have to do that for a living. She wanted me to go to school and get an education and become whatever I wanted to become."

Thriving in a predominately African American high school, Dolly learned early about the importance of working towards common ground. Participating in student government, she was elected student body president in her senior year.

For college, Dolly attended nearby UCLA. She double majored in Political Science and East Asian Studies. As a 4'11" college freshman, she became a coxswain for the women's crew team. She coxed her Novice 8 team to win the National Women's Rowing Association's southwestern regional championship, earning her the nickname "the Little General." She cofounded two Asian Pacific student organizations and coordinated celebrations for International Women's Day (March 8). In 1981, she graduated *summa cum laude* and Phi Beta Kappa.

Next, Dolly enrolled at UCLA School of Law. She jokingly called her mom her "first pro bono client," since Dolly routinely helped her as a translator. She recounted her mother

> … inspired my desire to go to law school, because I saw firsthand the difficulties that she encountered as a non-English speaker and also as a garment worker. I saw many abuses at her factory. I decided at a fairly early age that I wanted to do some type of work that would help to address some of the inequities that I saw as a child.

After graduating in 1984, Dolly clerked for two years for a federal district judge in Sacramento, California. Then she joined a Los Angeles law firm that represented employees and labor unions. Becoming a partner in 1990, she overcame clients' stereotypes arising from her diminutive stature and youthful appearance. Dolly reflected, "On many occasions during my career, I faced situations where I was the only woman or the only person of color in the room. I just did not allow that to be an impediment."

Dolly was president of the Southern California Chinese Lawyers Association in 1992. To build minority coalitions after the Los Angeles 1992 civil unrest, she co-founded the Multicultural Bar Alliance and the Asian Pacific American Bar Association. In 1994, President Bill Clinton appointed her to arbitrate and mediate disputes between labor unions and federal agencies.

Although America is increasingly diverse, the US judiciary was composed of white men for most of the 20th century. Dolly's friends urged her to consider joining the pool of applicants to become a federal judge. Despite being content in her law practice and having misgivings about changing her career path, Dolly applied. In 1999, Clinton nominated her late in his second term. Her nomination stalled in the US Senate and then lapsed after the 2000 election.

Ten years later, Dolly resubmitted her application, and in 2009, President Barack Obama re-nominated her. At Dolly's Senate confirmation hearing, California

Senator Barbara Boxer said, "as a daughter of immigrants from rural China, [Dolly] personifies the American dream. She used her position as a prominent attorney in Los Angeles to promote racial tolerance and fight for justice for those who face discrimination." On Christmas Eve 2009, Dolly was confirmed as the first Chinese American woman in the nation's history to become a federal judge under Article III of the Constitution.

After 9/11, the newly created Department of Homeland Security split the role of INS between Customs & Border Protection and Immigration & Customs Enforcement (ICE). As the political debate over "illegal aliens" became more polarized, the judiciary had to uphold the rule of law. In 2013, Dolly ruled that mentally disabled plaintiffs facing deportation must be provided legal representation in immigration court. In 2015, she denied the Obama administration's request to extend the detention period for undocumented minors, and affirmed that the FSA's standards applied to all detained migrant children, even those who arrived with parents. Investigations revealed that minors were detained in overcrowded and unsanitary conditions, which did not meet the FSA's requirements.

After the 2016 election, immigration issues became even more divisive. The Trump administration adopted controversial policies that banned travelers from Muslim countries,

"AN ERROR DOES NOT BECOME TRUTH BY REASON OF MULTIPLIED PROPAGATION, NOR DOES TRUTH BECOME ERROR BECAUSE NOBODY SEES IT."

— MAHATMA GANDHI

reduced the number of refugees accepted, and made it harder for immigrants to seek asylum. In 2017, it authorized a policy separating children from their detained parents. By the time the practice ended, this policy had affected more than three thousand children.

In 2017, Dolly ordered the return of an Iranian man, who had been granted permanent residence but was prevented from entering the United States under the travel ban. Later that year, she ruled that ICE deprived detained minors of necessities such as soap and toothbrushes, and FSA-mandated "safe and sanitary" conditions. In 2019, Dolly denied the Trump administration's proposal to detain children indefinitely in ICE facilities without court oversight. Rejecting the Justice Department's claims that these changes were consistent with the FSA, she countered, "Just because you tell me it's night outside doesn't mean it's not day."

The FSA ensures that our nation treats all migrant children in custody "with dignity, respect, and special concern for their particular vulnerability as minors." Dolly has scrutinized repeated attempts to undermine that standard.

Affirming the importance of actively participating in our society, Dolly commented, "If you do not have a voice at the table, there are many decisions that are made that may adversely affect your community."

SOURCES

www.congress.gov/111/chrg/shrg62345/CHRG-111shrg62345.htm

www.kqed.org/news/11777020/judge-rules-against-feds-on-regulations-that-would-detain-migrant-families-indefinitely

www.latimes.com/local/lanow/la-me-ln-lax-detained-iran-20170129-story.html

www.napaba.org/page/inspirationalseries

www.nytimes.com/2019/09/27/us/migrant-children-flores-court.html

# Dr. Jane Luu

## ASTRONOMER

Born: July 15, 1963          Saigon, Vietnam

**"If you're really interested in something, you're already halfway there."**

In 1975, Lưu Lệ Hằng was almost twelve years old when South Vietnam lost its war against the North and her family fled their home. Arriving in the United States as a refugee, she adopted the name Jane Luu. Around that time, NASA launched two Voyager probes to explore Mars and beyond. By 1986, Jane had become a naturalized American citizen and gotten a summer job at NASA's Jet Propulsion Laboratory (JPL) in Pasadena, California.

JPL was Voyager's headquarters and Voyager 2 was now closely approaching Uranus. Seeing photos of faraway, mysterious bodies, Jane recalled, "That was the first time I realized, 'Wow, there are people who go and study these things and do this for a living.'"

Many distinguished stargazers preceded Jane. In 1943, Irish scientist Kenneth Edgewood suggested that a pool of comets existed beyond our solar system. In 1951, Dutch astronomer Gerard Kuiper proposed this outer ring of frozen objects was beyond Pluto, fifty astronomical units away (AU is the distance from Earth to the sun). But since such objects would be so incredibly dim, no evidence was found and their notions forgotten.

Here on Earth, countries in Asia were fracturing in plain sight. After World War II, Communist Chinese overthrew the Nationalist government in 1949 and then battled the United States in Korea, splitting the latter in half in 1953. Meanwhile, rebels in Vietnam fought their French colonial masters, also dividing that country into two in 1954. In the following year, Jane's father Lu'u Xuong and mother Loi Phuong joined nearly one million people to migrate southward.

Born in South Vietnam, Jane was the second daughter and two more sons followed. The region was embroiled in another war in the 1960s, as the United States supported the South and China backed the North. Jane's father was an interpreter for the US Army while she studied French in school. When the United States withdrew its armed forces in 1973, the South soon fell. Jane's family escaped on one of the last planes leaving the country.

An aunt sponsored the family to go to Paducah, Kentucky and in 1976, Jane's family relocated to Ventura, California. Her father became a bookkeeper and her mother worked in an electronics factory. Learning English quickly, Jane won a scholarship to attend Stanford in 1980 and graduated with a Physics degree in 1984. After her epiphany at JPL, she enrolled in the Department of Earth, Atmospheric, and Planetary Science at MIT in 1986.

While Jane was looking for a research project, her doctorate advisor David Jewitt posed the question, "Why is the outer solar system so empty?"

**5430 Luu** IS AN ASTEROID (WITH A DIAMETER OF 7 KILOMETERS) BETWEEN MARS AND JUPITER THAT ORBITS THE SUN.

Together they sought proof for Edgewood's and Kuiper's conjectures by searching the night sky, even while Jane worked on her official thesis project of investigating the link between asteroids and comets.

In 1988, Jewitt went to the Institute for Astronomy at the University of Hawai'i and Luu followed. Coincidentally Kuiper had visited Hawai'i in 1963 (the year Luu was born) to survey a suitable site for a telescope. To revive the local economy after a 1960 tsunami, the Hawai'i Chamber of Commerce sought astronomers to help convince NASA to build an observatory there.

A sacred volcanic mountain on the big island, Mauna Kea had high altitude, dry climate, cloudless and dark skies, and clear visibility to observe the heavens. Kuiper was the only one who replied. Soon the summit hosted the most advanced stargazing equipment on the globe.

Graduating with her MIT PhD in 1990, Luu garnered the American Astronomical Society's 1991 Annie Jump Cannon Award for the most promising North American female astronomer. However, work with Jewitt on their "Slow Moving Objects Survey" had yielded no results thus far. Luu recalled:

> There was a joy in challenging conventional wisdom .... We begged, borrowed, or stole telescope time to keep looking, though people thought we were crazy.

March and September were months with windows for observations, so Luu and Jewitt would go use the best available telescopes, such as at Kitt Peak in Arizona. Previously, astronomers searched for solar system objects by photographing large areas of the sky with large glass plates coated by light-sensitive material. By comparing images taken of the same area, but separated by some time, they could detect objects moving slowly against this background.

Luu and Jewitt used the same technique, but with a new type of detector called charge-coupled devices (CCDs). Today CCD sensors are used in digital and video cameras to capture and convert light into data to record high resolution images.

Although Luu had become a Harvard-Smithsonian Postdoctoral Fellow at the Center for Astrophysics in Cambridge, Massachusetts, she continued working with Jewitt in Hawaiʻi. The team's breakthrough came at the University of Hawaiʻi's 2.2-meter telescope on Mauna Kea, which offered a bigger and better CCD. "Our procedure was to take three images of a region, each exposure taking fifteen minutes, and separated in time by an hour or so." Animating the frames on computers, they would see if an object moved.

On their second night using this improved camera, August 30, 1992, Luu and Jewett spotted something. They named it 1992 QB, and it was more than 150 miles in diameter. Disproving doubters, the two found 28 Kuiper Belt Objects (KBOs) in the next four years. Now more than 2,000 KBOs have been spotted. The total could be in the billions, depending on the size range used to classify them.

In 1994, Luu became an assistant professor at Harvard University. After four years, she left to teach at Leiden University in the Netherlands, where Kuiper had graduated with his PhD. There she met astronomer Ronnie Hoogerwerf and they married in 2001 in Los Osos, California. Luu missed America and her family. "I didn't want to get back into the rat race of academia," she reflected, so she joined MIT's Lincoln Laboratory in 2001. At this research center, she worked on satellite instruments, light detection and ranging (LiDAR) systems, and new detector technology.  Now she is a senior scientist at Draper Lab, where she is working on a lunar lander and projects involving LiDAR.

In 2006, Luu had a daughter named Eliot. In the same year, Pluto was downgraded to a dwarf planet and reclassified in hindsight as the first KBO discovered in 1930.

Six years later, astronomy's prestigious Kavli and Shaw prizes were awarded to both Jewitt and Luu for discovering the donut-shaped Kuiper Belt. The Shaw Prize selection committee wrote:

> Astronomy is arguably the oldest science. Observations of the motion of heavenly bodies date back more than 2,500 years. Nevertheless, as recently as 1992, immediately prior to the detection of the first Kuiper belt objects (KBOs) by Jewitt and Luu, little was known about the contents of the solar system beyond 30 AU.

Extending from Neptune (the fourth largest planet, almost 400% larger than Earth) to far beyond Pluto (which takes 248 years to orbit the sun), the Kuiper Belt is twenty times bigger than the asteroid belt (which lies between Mars and Jupiter). It could be home to more than a trillion comets. Containing leftover debris from when the solar system was formed 4.5 billion years ago, the Kuiper Belt also influenced the orbits of the outer planets.

In 2006, NASA launched the spacecraft *New Horizons*. It arrived at Pluto in 2015. Then on New Year's Day 2019, it flew by the KBO nicknamed Ultima Thule, the farthest object ever explored (more than four billion miles from Earth). NASA vehicles have been hard working and persistent, qualities that Luu values.

Back at Jane's first job at JPL, who would have guessed that an asteroid would be named after her a decade later? Jane commented:

> If you're interested in *something*, you care about it, think a lot about it, and then you're going to have good ideas. If you have some perseverance and you stick to your ideas, you can make something of them.

In the meantime, the skies kept beckoning. In 2017, Jewitt and Luu used the Nordic Optical Telescope in the Canary Islands to investigate 'Oumuamua (Hawaiian for "scout"), the first interstellar object observed passing through the solar system. Then in 2019, they tracked Borisov, the first detected interstellar comet.

SOURCES
http://imagiverse.org/interviews/janeluu/jane_luu_21_03_03.htm
http://shawprize.org
https://hyphenmagazine.com/blog/2009/3/31/womens-history-month-profile-jane-luu
https://napawf.org/womens-history-month/2019/3/20/jane-luu
www.nytimes.com/2018/12/30/science/nasa-new-horizons-kuiper-belt.html
www.sciencemag.org/careers/2012/10/no-starry-eyed-astronomer

# Satya Nadella

## TECHNOLOGIST & CEO

Born: August 19, 1967          Andhra Pradesh, India

"I'm the product of two amazing, unique American things. American technology
that reached me where I was growing up, helped me dream the dream,
and then the enlightened American immigration policy that let me come
here and live the dream. So when I think about it, only in America
would a story like mine even be possible."

The company press release was about to hit the wire. Soon the whole world would know. The days
of toiling in the shadows of giants were over. With the spotlight on him, his every word would be
scrutinized. Satya Nadella's life was about to change forever.

On February 4, 2014, Microsoft named Nadella their third Chief Executive Officer (CEO). In 1975, Bill Gates dropped out of Harvard College to found the company with Paul Allen. In 1980, they hired Steve Ballmer as employee #30 and their first business manager. Soon Microsoft dominated the global personal computing (PC) market with its text-based Microsoft Disk Operating System (MS-DOS). In 1983, Microsoft released their graphics-based Windows operating system, and in 1989, Microsoft launched their Office software suite. By 1995 when it offered Internet Explorer as a web browser, Microsoft had 90+% market share of PCs worldwide and Bill Gates had become the richest person in the world with $12.9 billion. Rebelling against Microsoft's iron grip on the market, critics compared it to the Evil Empire in the movie *Star Wars* and asked the US government to fine it as a monopoly.

In 2000, the burly Ballmer became CEO. Microsoft's revenues tripled and profits doubled. Gates' net worth was $60 billion. Allen used his fortune to buy (among other things) NBA's Portland Trail Blazers, the NFL's Seattle Seahawks, and a stake in the Seattle Sounders Major League Soccer (MLS) team. But in the 21st century of the Internet and cell phones, Microsoft's stock price languished as competitors such as Apple, Google, Amazon, and Facebook surged ahead online.

Many industry pundits thought Microsoft's best days were behind it. However, Nadella believed otherwise. He had emerged victorious after a grueling six-month executive search process. In the bigger scheme of things, the opportunity of a lifetime laid ahead.

Bukkapuram Nadella Satyanarayana Chowdary was born in the state of Andhra Pradesh in south-central India. His father was a government administrator and his mother was a college professor in the ancient Indian language of Sanskrit. When Nadella was six, his baby sister died, so his mother became a homemaker. After moving many times for his father's jobs, the family settled in the capital city and Nadella boarded at the Hyderabad Public School.

Admittedly "not academically great," he earned an Electrical Engineering degree from the Manipal Institute of Technology in 1988. Then he traveled to the United States to get a Master's Degree in Computer Science from the University of Wisconsin at Milwaukee in 1990.

In 1992, Nadella gained admission to the Masters in Business Administration (MBA) Program at the University of Chicago, joined Microsoft, and married Anupama Priyadarshini, an architect and family friend from India. Reunited in Redmond, Washington, their life was moving at full speed when suddenly they hit a roadblock.

In 1996, the couple welcomed their first son Zain. Unfortunately, Zain suffered from lack of oxygen in Anupama's womb. The newborn had spastic quadriplegia cerebral palsy (the inability to control one's whole body), and was legally blind. Nadella recalled, "I was devastated. But mostly, I was sad for how things turned out for me and Anu. Thankfully, Anu helped me to understand that it was not about what happened to me."

> … [I]t was my son who needed the help. And I needed to show up as a father and in some sense do my job and do my duty — but more importantly, see the world through his eyes. You may say, well, these are all things that happen in personal life, but I've come to realize that if you think about creating anything new, any new product, any new business, as a leader, the one skill that you need more than any other skill is that deep sense of empathy.

Two daughters, Tara and Divya, followed. One had special needs. For five years, the family would shuttle between her specialized school in Vancouver, Canada and Zain's caregivers in Seattle. Through these experiences, Nadella realized:

> I discovered that recognition of these universal predicaments leads to universal empathy — empathy for and among children, adults, parents, and teachers. Empathy, we learned, was indivisible and was a universal value. And we learned that empathy is essential to deal with problems everywhere, whether at Microsoft or at home; here in the United States or globally. That is also a mindset, a culture.

When Nadella joined Microsoft, he was one of just a few dozen Indian American employees. His career continued its ascent and in 2013, he supervised the company's "cloud" (online services) division. Now his job was to lead by "bringing clarity, bringing energy, and ultimately

Because of my own experience, and by learning from my colleagues, I get now how hard it is to join a company that doesn't look like you and to live in a community where most of your neighbors don't look like you. How do you identify role models you can fully relate to? How do you find mentors, coaches, and sponsors who can help you succeed without hiding your true self? At work, the tech industry, including Microsoft, is simply not as diverse as we must become. And outside work, minorities can also feel isolated.... We all want a culture in which we're heard and supported.

Regrettably, employees and their employers are under stress like never before. In 2020, as the coronavirus spread in Washington state, Microsoft quickly had most of its employees work from home. The *New York Times* wrote that the company was "ahead of the pack" in adjusting to the crisis by transitioning to telecommuting. Countless businesses nationwide had to close. By June 2020, more than forty million people filed for unemployment — one in four working Americans. This was the highest percentage since the 1929 Great Depression.

"As COVID-19 impacts every aspect of our work and life, we have seen two years' worth of digital transformation in two months," Nadella responded. Now he must lead his company to assist "customers every day to help them stay open for business in a world of remote everything."

SOURCES

https://news.uchicago.edu/story/chicago-booth-visit-microsoft-ceo-discusses-what-he-looks-leader

https://qz.com/work/1539071/how-microsoft-ceo-satya-nadella-rebuilt-the-company-culture/

www.bloomberg.com/news/features/2019-05-02/satya-nadella-remade-microsoft-as-world-s-most-valuable-company

www.cnet.com/news/this-is-not-your-fathers-microsoft/

www.goodhousekeeping.com/life/inspirational-stories/a46221/satya-anu-nadella-microsoft/

# Lea Salonga

## SINGER

Born: February 22, 1971    Angeles, Pampanga, Philippines

*"The only thing we can do is keep on creating more stories and to not take this moment for granted and to keep grinding away and to keep writing and still keep filming and bringing specific points of view out to the public for people to see."*

In 1712, Frenchman Antoine Galland translated a collection of Middle Eastern stories into *1001 Nights: Arabian Tales*. Volumes 9 through 12, published after his death, contained the bonus story of "Aladdin or the Wonderful Lamp." The original fable is set in China where a tailor's son likes the married princess Badroulbadour. But Disney's 1992 animated version changed the country and characters, and added songs and a magic carpet. Soaring on a rug in the sky, the lovebirds croon a memorable duet.

Lea Salonga provided the singing voice of Princess Jasmine. The song "A Whole New World" won the Grammy Award for Song of the Year and Academy Award for Best Original Song. But Lea had already been flying around the globe and fulfilling her dreams, fueled by the power of her voice.

Maria Lea Carmen Imutan Salonga was born in 1971, in central Luzon, the main island of the Philippines. In this Pacific archipelago of 7,641 islands, Lea's father was a naval officer, maritime engineer, and shipyard director. Her brother Gerard was born two years later and in 1977, the family moved to the capital city of Manila.

Lea started singing professionally at age seven in *The King and I*. After playing the lead in *Annie*, she released her first album *Small Voice* when she was ten. Lea recalled, "We peddled my music, going from music store to music store. It didn't happen overnight. What does? Then, the orders were coming in — more than we ever imagined."

Soon, Lea began winning awards for best child performer. In 1983, she hosted her own musical television show *Love, Lea*. The teen idol was grounded by her mom Ligaya, who would eventually chaperone her daughter around the world. Lea remembered:

[Mom] knew how much I loved rehearsals and that environment — being on stage. One condition was to finish my homework first before a rehearsal or to bring it with me to rehearsals. I think that was just a motivation for me to keep my "academics" up.

By 1988, after releasing her second album, Lea was studying Biology at the University of Ateneo de Manila and Theater Arts at the University of the Philippines. Meanwhile an upcoming British production had already auditioned more than 1,000 girls in London, New York, Los Angeles, and Hawai'i for a major role. The casting directors went to Manila. Lea tried out. After three days, she won the part.

A year later, Lea made her London West End debut in *Miss Saigon*. Set during the Vietnam War, a Vietnamese girl Kim falls in love with an American soldier, but suffers heartbreaking tragedy. Lea recollected, "I would rather think of all the good stuff that came out of it, but it was definitely a lot of pressure to put on an eighteen-year-old. It was crazy, nuts."

One problem was that Salonga had little formal voice training. In retrospect she noted,

> Musical theater might as well be classified as an athletic sport. It takes so much physical stamina, it takes so much mental energy, vocal stamina as well. It's like your entire body is wrecked by the time the eight shows a week are done. Physical therapy is a necessity.

In England the intense daily strain soon damaged Lea's vocal cords. "The doctor said I needed to heal and rest. So I was silent for a week and a half to two weeks." But with the help of coach Mary Hammond, she recovered:

> [Mary] took it apart and put it back together again. She changed the whole technique of how I sang. Over a year, I went to her once a week and she fixed my voice. I have not had any major troubles since seeing her because of how she taught me then …. I am always grateful to that woman for everything she did. That voice people are familiar with after *Miss Saigon* … is thanks to her.

At the same time, Lea noticed a sign to guide her future. On a night off from work, she and her mother attended a Catholic church service.

> … [T]his priest who was visiting had only a couple of sentences in his homily, and he said, "We have all been given gifts by God. Use the gifts that God gave you." And that was my moment. That was when I realized "I am exactly where I am supposed to be. I'm doing exactly what it is I'm supposed to be doing for the rest of my life."

*Miss Saigon* was a British theatrical success and Lea won the Laurence Olivier Award for Best Actress. Two years later, she went to New York to reprise her role. On Broadway, she became the first Asian woman to win a Tony Award for Best Actress.

Despite her star turn, Lea remembered when "I was told I couldn't be seen for *My Fair Lady* because I was Asian." Nevertheless in 1992, Lea was the first Asian to play the teenager

Eponine in *Les Misérables*, based on Victor Hugo's epic novel about France's June Rebellion of 1832. Lea returned to portray the single mother Fantine in the 2007 Broadway revival.

In 1998, Disney again cast her to sing in another hit animated movie, *Mulan*. In the song "Reflection," Mulan rebels against social expectations for women in ancient China. Lea recounted,

> Because these films are easy to access, there are many generations of children that have seen both movies and I got to play two princesses that were people of colour… they have a lot of young women look to them, heroes, strong and somewhat influential in their own way.

Following her participation in the revival of *Flower Drum Song* in 2002, she married Robert Chien in 2004. Two years later, they had a daughter Nicole. Aptly, Lea provided the voice of Mrs. Kusakabe (mother of the energetic girls Satsuki and Mei) in Disney's 2010 English release of Hayao Miyazaki's beloved animated film *My Neighbor Totoro*. The next year Disney inducted her into their hall of fame as a "Disney Legend."

Also in 2011, Lea began singing cabaret, and toured the world regularly in one-woman shows while performing in other media. Back home in the Philippines, in 2013, she judged on their

version of the television show *The Voice* and added *The Voice Kids* the following year. In 2015, she played Kei Kimura in the Broadway production of George Takei's *Allegiance* which is about a Japanese American family enduring internment in World War II. Then in 2018 on Broadway, Lea played Erzulie, the Goddess of Love, in *Once on This Island*, which won a Tony Award for Best Revival of a Musical.

Lea returned to cinema in the 2019 independent film *Yellow Rose*. She played the Texas aunt of Rose, a seventeen-year-old Filipina American whose dream of becoming a country music singer is interrupted when ICE arrests her mother for being an illegal alien. Two years before, the young lead, Eva Noblezada, had earned a 2017 Tony nomination for her role as Kim in the Broadway revival of *Miss Saigon*.

Continuing its strategy of remaking its popular animated films into live-action, Disney launched a revised *Aladdin* in 2019. Next, it produced a new $200 million version of *Mulan*, this time with an all-Asian cast. However, before *Mulan*'s cinematic release in 2020, the coronavirus pandemic turned off the lights of theaters worldwide.

According to a 2017 report by the Asian American Performers Action Coalition, although Asians were 12.7% of New York City's population, only 7.3% of its theaters' casts were Asian.

Given that underrepresentation, Filipinos consider Lea a living national treasure and an inspirational role model. In 2020, she performed for Bayanihan Musikahan's livestreamed fundraising concerts to provide food for the poor in the Philippines imperiled by the COVID-19 quarantine.

Artists are not just entertainers. Lea reflected:

> As performers, part of our job is to step into another person's shoes and see what it must be like to live a lifetime in them in the span of a couple of hours. The characters we play allow our audience to see things through someone else's eyes — and, hopefully, help trigger a change.

When Hollywood and Broadway's lights turn on again, more in the arts should reflect upon the parts Asians can truly play.

SOURCES

https://leasalonga.com

www.broadwayworld.com/chicago/article/-BWW-Interview-Broadway-veteran-Lea-Salonga-reflects-on-her-touring-and-Broadway-experiences-20190424

www.teenvogue.com/story/lea-salonga-yellow-rose-disney-interview

www.thestage.co.uk/features/interviews/2019/lea-salonga-the-physical-demands-on-musical-theatre-performers-are-crazy/

www.townandcountry.ph/people/inspiration/lea-salonga-cover-story-october-2018

# DWAYNE "THE ROCK" JOHNSON

## WRESTLER & ACTOR

Born: May 2, 1972          Hayward, California

*"There was a time in my life when opportunities were so few and far between they were like little cracks in the wall, and if one opportunity came my way, I would scratch and claw and bite and I would do anything I could to make sure that I grabbed that opportunity by the throat and I did not let it go."*

After his father died, Wayde Bowles fought his mother's boyfriend and left home when he was fourteen. With a few dollars in his pocket, he hitchhiked one thousand miles from Nova Scotia, Canada to Toronto. He hit the gym and later changed his name to Rocky Johnson to honor boxers Rocky Marciano and Jack

Johnson. Becoming a wrestler with charisma, muscles, and fancy footwork, Rocky paired with Tony Atlas in 1983 to become the first African American tag team champions of the World Wrestling Federation (WWF, now WWE). They dethroned the Wild Samoans, the brothers Afa and Sika Anoa'i, who held twenty-one team titles. Ironically, the Anoa'is' dad was blood brother with Rocky's father-in-law Peter Maivia. Chief of his clan, Maivia was the first Samoan wrestling star and battled Sean Connery's James Bond in the 1967 film *You Only Live Twice*.

Grappling for more than twenty years, Rocky would mold his son Dwayne into an even more magnetic entertainer. After playing high school football in Pennsylvania, Dwayne attended the University of Miami. The 6'3" freshman was a defensive tackle on the Hurricanes, which won the National Collegiate Athletic Association (NCAA) 1991 championship. But "Dewey" lost his starting spot to future NFL Hall of Famer Warren Sapp and got injured his senior year. Graduating in 1995, undrafted by the NFL, Dwayne tried out for the Canadian Football League (CFL). Cut by the Calgary Stampeders, he asked his dad to drive him home to Tampa, Florida, and wondered what to do next.

As a child, Dwayne watched his high-flying father. He practiced being interviewed by replaying wrestling tapes on a videocassette player. Now Dwayne asked his dad to train him. Rocky refused. Then he relented and literally gave Dwayne a crash course. Dwayne began in the minor leagues as "Flex Cabana," earning $40 per match. Soon the WWF called him "Rocky Maivia" (as the first 3rd generation pro wrestler) and cast him in 1996's *Survivor Series* at New York's Madison Square Garden.

In 1997, Dwayne won his first title, Intercontinental Champion, besting Hunter Hearst Helmsley (aka Triple H) and then shared the ring with his father at *WrestleMania 13*. But Dwayne's smiling babyface (good guy) persona did not go "over" (wrestling slang for convincing fans to care about you). In hindsight, Dwayne called this the turning point in his life. Struggling to find his identity, he had to "be myself" and "be authentic."

Later that year, Dwayne married Dany Garcia and turned into a brash, outspoken heel (bad guy) with a new moniker. In 2000, his autobiography *The Rock Says…* was a number one *New York Times* bestseller and he spoke at the Republican National Convention. His daughter Simone was born in the next year and The Rock has been on a wild ride ever since.

Dwayne's adult success is a far cry from his troubled youth. As a teenager growing up in Hawai'i, he was a thief and had problems with the law. His family was evicted from their

$180 / week apartment when he was fourteen and his mother attempted suicide when he was fifteen. He brooded, "How can I avoid this?" By junior high school, he had lived in more than a dozen states.

Dwayne's first acting job was in 1999 when he impersonated his father on ABC TV's *That '70s Show*. "Rocky" pronounced, "I got a son and one day he's gonna become the most electrifying man in sports entertainment." But Dwayne did not like acting at first and refused to go on NBC's television comedy show *Saturday Night Live* (*SNL*). Finally, he agreed to host in 2000. Then Hollywood beckoned. He had a bit part in 2001's *The Mummy Returns*. Quickly he entered the *Guinness Book of World Records* for the highest salary earned by a first-time lead actor, $5.5 million to headline the 2002 prequel *The Scorpion King*.

Though divorced in 2007, Dany remained a good friend and they started Seven Bucks Productions in 2012: that's how much Dwayne had in his wallet when he left the CFL. Together they produced HBO's *Ballers* (Dwayne played a retired NFL player who managed other athletes' finances) and NBC's *Titan Games* (a gladiator-like athletic competition). He collaborated with Under Armour on stylish active wear. The first Project Rock shoe sold out in 2018 and an apparel line was launched in 2019.

Pro wrestlers tell a story with their moves and their mouths. The Rock mastered the microphone with catch phrases to create a larger than life stage presence. Raising his right eyebrow, he incited fans by intoning, "if you smell what the Rock is cooking." The People's Champion flashed finishing moves: The Rock Bottom body slam and The People's Elbow drop. Nicknaming himself "The Great One" and referring himself in the third person, the Brahma Bull likely coined the word "smackdown" that is listed in the dictionary.

In the squared circle, The Rock feuded with "Stone Cold" Steve Austin, Kurt Angle, and Mick Foley. He won seventeen title belts, including heavyweight champ ten times. His grappling Samoan "cousins" included Haku, Yokozuna, Tamina Snuka (daughter of Jimmy "Superfly" Snuka), Rikishi (whose sons competed as the Uso brothers), Roman Reigns, and Nia Jax. In 2008, he inducted both his father and grandfather (who died in 1982) into the WWE Hall of Fame.

On the mat, The Rock has taken many "bumps." Wrestling may be choreographed with a scripted result, but injuries take their toll. Tangling with John Cena at *WrestleMania 29*, The Rock tore his abductor muscle, suffered a hernia, and needed emergency surgery. As an actor, Dwayne does not do his own stunts but gets better pay. His pictures include *Rampage*, the *Fast & Furious* franchise, and *Jumanji*. After watching The Rock in *The Tooth Fairy*, actor Hugh Jackman got workout and diet advice to play Wolverine in the *X-Men* superhero films.

Not all of The Rock's forty-plus films are acclaimed by critics. To use one of Dwayne's slogans, it doesn't matter. His audiences — and buddy costars Kevin Hart and Jason Statham — like him. In 2016, *People* magazine named Dwayne the "Sexiest Man Alive" and *Forbes* ranked him the world's highest paid actor ($64 million) and again in 2019 ($89 million). Nowadays, he owns luxury cars, estates in Georgia and Virginia, and a $300,000 home gym. He trains everyday and transports his 40,000-pound personal weight room to his filming locations.

Dwayne's tattoos remind him of his roots. For the 2016 animated *Moana*, Disney hooked him as the voice of the morphing demigod Maui, whose character design was inspired by Dwayne's grandfather. Representing his

"YOU BROKE COLOR BARRIERS, BECAME A RING LEGEND AND TRAIL BLAZED YOUR WAY THRU THIS WORLD. I WAS THE BOY SITTING IN THE SEATS, WATCHING AND ADORING YOU, MY HERO FROM AFAR. THE BOY YOU RAISED TO ALWAYS BE PROUD OF OUR CULTURES AND PROUD OF WHO AND WHAT I AM. THE BOY YOU RAISED WITH THE TOUGHEST OF LOVE. THE INTENSE WORK. THE HARD HAND. THE ADORING BOY WHO WANTED TO KNOW ONLY YOUR BEST QUALITIES. WHO THEN GREW TO BECOME A MAN REALIZING YOU HAD OTHER DEEPLY COMPLICATED SIDES THAT NEEDED TO BE HELD AND UNDERSTOOD. SON TO FATHER. MAN TO MAN. THAT'S WHEN MY ADORATION TURNED TO RESPECT. AND MY EMPATHY TURNED TO GRATITUDE. GRATEFUL THAT YOU GAVE ME LIFE. GRATEFUL YOU GAVE ME LIFE'S INVALUABLE LESSONS."

— DWAYNE JOHNSON (@THEROCK),
  JANUARY 17, 2020

Pacific Islander heritage, he said, "The opportunity that we had, just as Polynesians, to be part of a story and to bring to life a story of our Polynesian culture … [was] really, really special." In his 2019 movie *Hobbs and Shaw*, Dwayne included the Samoan war dance the *siva tau*. He recalled his mother Ata Maivia crying on the set: "It was our way of paying homage and honoring a culture that I'm very proud of, and that has been responsible for teaching me defining values throughout the years."

Not forgetting his alma mater, in 2007 Dwayne donated $1 million to Miami's Athletic Department. Then in 2013, the Hurricanes named its new football locker room after him. Later, The Rock participated in the Make-A-Wish Foundation and joined the *SNL* Five-Timers Club in 2017.

Dwayne married a second time in 2019 to Lauren Hashian in Hawai'i, and had two daughters (Jasmine in 2015 and Tiana in 2018). Seven Bucks produced *Fighting with My Family*, a movie where Dwayne plays The Rock who helps a girl to become a pro wrestler. In 2020, his daughter Simone began training at the WWE's Performance Center in Orlando, Florida.

Then on January 15, 2020, Rocky Johnson died of a heart attack. Oprah Winfrey interviewed Dwayne a few weeks later. He reflected on the complicated relationship with his father, who dispensed tough love but was "proud when I became successful in an industry he had given his life to."

Mindful of his upcoming movies (Disney's *Jungle Cruise*, Netflix's *Red Notice*, and DC Comics' *Black Adam*), Dwayne affirmed his goal was "to create an amazing experience for people" and address "how can I send the audience home happy and make people feel good." Spoken like a true entertainer whose motto is "the show must go on."

SOURCES

*Oprah Winfrey: 2020 Vision Tour.* www.youtube.com/watch?v=btcuxx2mjfA

*Rocky Johnson Interview.* www.youtube.com/watch?v=eWXbQudEz4Y

www.espn.com/blog/playbook/fandom/post/_/id/15186/how-good-was-the-rock-at-football

www.esquire.com/entertainment/interviews/a36037/dwayne-johnson-the-rock-0815/

www.latimes.com/entertainment-arts/movies/story/2019-07-25/dwayne-johnson-speaks-samoan-fast-and-furious-hobbs-and-shaw

# DAVID CHANG

## CHEF & RESTAURATEUR

Born: August 5, 1977                    Vienna, Virginia

**"Asian American food, Asian food in general, is not the predominant food
and it's going to be widely misunderstood .... If someone wants to talk about it,
and promote it — fine. All I ask is that it's respectful. All I ask is that they pay tribute
and understand it and [the food is] an homage to where it came from."**

A world renowned chef, television host, and tastemaker, David Chang has expressed, "I just want something that's delicious." His career took off in 2004, when he named his first New York restaurant after Momofuku Ando, who founded the Japanese food manufacturer Nissin and was credited for popularizing instant ramen. Momofuku can be translated to mean "lucky peach." But David's culinary triumphs are more than luck. He has changed the way people look at food.

David's parents emigrated from Korea. Arriving practically penniless in New York, his father Joe got his first job washing dishes. Later he and his wife Sherri moved to a Washington, DC suburb where they opened a deli. Growing up with older brothers and a sister, David loved his mom's cooking but loathed it at school when others made fun of his lunch. Meanwhile his "tiger dad" groomed David to become a golf prodigy at the age of five. He became a state champion but burned out by middle school.

It would take David another decade to find his calling, He majored in Religion at Trinity College in Connecticut. Graduating in 1999, he taught English in Japan for a few months and returned to New York's French Culinary Institute. In 2001, he worked at the fine dining establishments of Mercer Kitchen and Craft. Reassessing his existence after 9/11, David went back to Japan which "changed my life." Laboring in kitchens for two years, he learned to love Japanese food and the passion, skill, and discipline required to create it.

Coming home, David convinced his parents and their friends to lend him $130,000 to open a noodle bar. He was a cursing workaholic, struggling to survive. "Everything has to be right. It's a battle to find the details." In retrospect, "we were in the right place at the right time." Momofuku led a new wave of handmade ramen joints. The restaurant's 2009 cookbook, co-written by Peter Meehan, instantly became a bestseller.

David's customers savor food that's a little familiar, fancy, and fresh. Gochujang-marinated pork, curry crab, dashi-seasoned tofu, and other Asian ingredients get his yummy treatment. Not satisfied to simply serve good food, he also gives from his heart. David has supported the food rescue organization City Harvest and the Sierra Club. He has donated to Chef Alice Water's Edible Schoolyard, Sickkids (a children's hospital in Toronto, Canada where David has a restaurant), and Yale's Sustainable Food Project.

David made his own sauces and seasonings and now his restaurants do too. Founded in 2010, his Culinary Lab is a "research kitchen dedicated to exploring our culinary traditions and understanding the origins of flavor." Fermenting grains and concocting savory condiments reflect David: a dash of science, a smidge of style, and a soup ladle of hard work.

In Manhattan, David's footprint has stretched from Wall Street to South Street Seaport and Hudson Yards. Now his company network spans six American cities, and extends into Canada (entering Vancouver in 2020) and Australia (Seibo in Sydney). That means he also has a huge staff that believes in him.

No longer just concocting delectable dishes, David is making television shows. On Netflix he hosted the first 2012 season of *Mind of a Chef* (produced and narrated by the late chef Anthony Bourdain), investigating how flavorful food from sushi to bacon are made.

In 2018, he created the Netflix series *Ugly Delicious*, covering cravings from pizza to fried chicken. David explained, "The whole idea of ugly-delicious was, how do I make food that I'm comfortable making again? As I've gotten older, I've embraced all the things that I truly love eating. I'm not embarrassed about it anymore." In 2019, he debuted *Breakfast, Lunch & Dinner*. In the meantime, he was a guest judge on Bravo TV's *Top Chef: All Stars* and had a cameo on HBO's *Treme*.

Dining with Anthony Bourdain.

David has taken his lumps, though. In 2011, he launched Lucky Peach media which published cookbooks and an award-winning magazine, considered "beloved and pioneering" (*New York Times*) and "deliciously hip" (*Time* magazine), but closed it in 2017. He invested in a food delivery app Maple that folded the same year. In 2018, David's food delivery restaurant Ando and Midtown restaurant Ma Peche shuttered. Another restaurant Nishi got a mixed review from the *New York Times*. That criticism motivated him to improve it and give his chefs everywhere the freedom to innovate.

"There's something honest about getting better every day," David said. That is good advice, and not just for cooks. David does not want to be the only one trying new things. He wants his employees to grow too, and take field trips and classes that provide unexpected experiences. In 2005, he hired Christina Tosi to manage his operations. She became his pastry chef and then he incubated her desert shop Milk Bar in 2008.

Three years later, David hired Marguerite Mariscal (whose family owns the renowned New York specialty food store Zabar's) as an intern. In 2019, he promoted her to be CEO (his boss). Now David encourages colleagues "to fail in order to succeed" — only by making mistakes can they attain bigger goals.

As David influences new chefs, he remembers his journey. He admitted, "I wasn't that great," when talking about his early days of exploring Japan and contemplating his future. "I needed to challenge myself." Starting his own business, David was often clueless. "Because we sort of had nothing, we could question everything," he said to the *Washington Post*. "I guess I get irritated when people … don't find their own voice. Do you have your voice in your food in some way?" That deep desire to "personalize" his food helped him elevate his game.

Along the way, David rediscovered his pride in Korean food, from kimchi (fermented cabbage) to kimbap (seaweed wrapped sushi rolls). Six James Beard Foundation Awards (and six more nominations) later, his future seems limitless. Thanks to those professional accolades, there was no bigger name in food at the beginning of the 21st century.

As much as David loves to cook, he likes to eat and talk too. In 2017, he married Grace Seo, moved to Los Angeles to launch his restaurant Majordomo, and named a new media company after it. In 2018, for the Winter Olympics in Pyeongchang, South Korea, he was NBC's food correspondent (winning another Beard media award). Meanwhile he started his eponymous podcast, part of sportswriter Bill Simmons' Ringer network. David has recorded more than one hundred episodes, opining with noteworthy guests on all topics from cooking to culture.

In David's 2020 memoir *Eat a Peach*, "[h]e explains the ideas that guide him and demonstrates how cuisine is a weapon against complacency and racism." It also addresses his struggles with depression. Consulting with a psychiatrist since 2003, David called it "the longest relationship I've ever been in." Running Momofuku, he acknowledged that "I didn't sign a ten-year extension to the restaurant lease, since I didn't plan on living past thirty-five." Prompted by the 2018 suicide of "Uncle Tony" Bourdain, David confronts the daily challenge of maintaining his self-worth, and not be a slave to others' approval or his own success. He advocates for better mental health treatment in the restaurant industry and beyond.

Having his son Hugo in 2019 rekindled David's passion for cooking and renewed his purpose to nourish others. His mission is to not only demystify cooking for the masses and stand up for authentic ethnic cuisine, but also to make food that just tastes fantastic. "When you eat something amazing, you don't just respond to the dish in front of you; you are almost always transported back to another moment in your life."

The 2020 pandemic realized David's greatest phobia. In a 2008 interview in *The New Yorker*, he confessed, "It's not that I'm not happy; I'm just fearful for the future, I'm fearful that everything's gonna be taken away." Twelve years later, governments around the globe enforced social distancing and sheltering-in-place. David had to close sixteen locations (including two permanently) and lay off eight hundred employees, and said, "It's been the hardest couple weeks of my life." Calling mom-and-pop restaurants "too small to fail," David predicted, "Without government intervention, there will be no service industry."

Some forecast that most locally-owned businesses will not survive. Now one of the biggest proponents of Korean cuisine and the rich flavor of umami, David continues forward, encouraging people to value themselves and others through the shared love of food.

SOURCES
*The Dave Chang Show.* Ringer Podcast Network. www.theringer.com/the-dave-chang-show
*The Mind of a Chef, Ugly Delicious, and Breakfast, Lunch, Dinner.* Netflix.
www.newyorker.com/magazine/2008/03/24/chef-on-the-edge
www.nytimes.com/interactive/2020/03/27/magazine/david-chang-restaurants-covid19.html
www.washingtonpost.com/graphics/2019/lifestyle/food/david-chang/

# MINDY KALING

## WRITER, ACTRESS, & PRODUCER

Born: June 24, 1979          Cambridge, Massachusettes

*"Write your own part. It is the only way I've gotten anywhere. It is much harder work, but sometimes you have to take destiny into your own hands."*

Quotable Mindy Kaling has made her own breaks. Contributing to television shows like *The Office*, she has changed the comedy climate. Her rise may have been a surprise to everyone but herself.

Growing up, I definitely thought it was sociably acceptable for boys to be funny; that there was something not feminine about being funny, and that sticks with you. As a comedian, you always talk about that wound you had as a child, and you source your comedy from that.

Punch lines and laugh tracks aside, she said,

> The fact that I was interested in comedy as a girl at that age was already so strange to people. On top of that, I was a kid of Indian immigrants, who were not involved in the niche industry of comedy writing or acting. I have to give my parents credit for being incredibly supportive — and I am talking about nearly twenty years ago. I think their encouragement came from their own sense of adventure.

In the 1970s, Tamil architect Avu Chokalingam worked at a hospital in Nigeria and met Swati Roysircar, a Bengali obstetrician / gynecologist (OB / GYN). They came to America and settled in Cambridge, Massachusetts, where they had a son Vijay and a daughter Vera Mindy (named after the 1980s television sitcom *Mork and Mindy*).

As a child, Mindy waited at her mom's office after school and wrote stories on a typewriter. At home, she liked funny television shows. At the private school Buckingham Browne & Nichols, Mindy was "extremely bad at anything athletic," learned Latin, and was the "friendly, chubby nerd." Looking back, she concluded, "What I've noticed is that almost no one who was a big star in high school is also a big star in life. For us overlooked kids, it's so wonderfully *fair*."

Admitted to Dartmouth (Hanover, New Hampshire), Mindy sang a capella, performed improv, and drew newspaper cartoons. As a sophomore, she was a summer script intern at the Manhattan television show *Late Night*, hosted by her "comedy hero" Conan O'Brien. Now a regular guest on Conan's shows, she told him, "You represent to writers who want to be performers, you're proof of their potential."

Graduating in Playwriting in 2001, Mindy wanted to "make it" in the Big Apple. In Brooklyn, she roomed with two college pals.

However, getting a job was difficult after 9/11. Mindy babysat, assisted a television psychic, and tried stand-up comedy. After club comics mispronounced her last name, she shortened it to Kaling.

Inspired by the actors Matt Damon and Ben Affleck, Mindy and her roommate Brenda Withers wrote their own satire, *Matt and Ben*: the film script for *Good Will Hunting* (1998 Oscar winning screenplay) drops from the sky into their apartment. Directing themselves and wearing Brenda's brothers' clothes, the women won the 2002 New York Fringe Festival's best play. That led to a deal to make a Hollywood television pilot about themselves, *Mindy and Brenda*.

In Los Angeles they had to audition for their own roles. Ironically, Mindy joked that they "were not considered attractive or funny enough to play ourselves." In 2005, the pilot did not get picked up . . . but Mindy did.

Greg Daniels was producing NBC's version of the British television comedy *The Office* and had seen *Matt and Ben*. Daniels hired Mindy, the only woman among eight writers, and mentored her. In Episode 2, Mindy played the chatty Kelly Kapoor who slaps her selfish boss played by Steve Carrell (she also played one of Carrell's first dates in his hit film *The 40-Year-Old Virgin*). Eventually Kelly falls for a character played by B.J. Novak, another *The Office* writer who became Mindy's best buddy.

In *The Office*'s third season, Mindy wrote the first American comedy episode about the holiday Diwali, and her own parents played Kelly's mom and dad. "I was a little embarrassed with how little I knew about it. I'm Hindu, but I'm not really a practicing Hindu, so I had to do a lot of research," Mindy confessed. After an unsuccessful tryout for *Saturday Night Live (SNL)*, back at *The Office*, this "workaholic" wrote twenty-two episodes, and became a producer, director, and the first woman of color nominated for an Emmy in comedy writing.

In 2011, Mindy's first book of humorous essays *Everyone Hanging Out Without Me?* was an instant bestseller. Meanwhile she got an NBC development deal to create her own show. However, in 2012, just as Fox accepted Mindy's pitch, her mother died of pancreatic cancer at the hospital where she had worked for thirty years. Mindy forged ahead to be the first woman of color to both run and star in her own US network program. In *The Mindy Project*, Dr. Mindy Lahiri is an OB/GYN, a character inspired by Kaling's mother and by the last name of author Jhumpa Lahiri.

The single-camera comedy ran six seasons (three on Hulu). Managing a staff of 150, Mindy had more responsibility and freedom:

> All the best parts are people with spiky sides and nuances and contradictions in their lives. So, the way that I've come to terms with it, is that I hope that young women look to me…as a role model and let me play the characters I want to play.

That spirit got Mindy cast to voice car racer Taffyta Muttonfudge in the animation *Wreck-It Ralph*, and named one of *Time* magazine's "100 Most Influential People" as well as one of *Glamour* magazine's "Women of the Year" in 2014.

In 2015, Mindy dedicated her second bestseller *Why Not Me?* to her mother. In it, she reels off one-liners but also addresses her body image: "Though I am generally a happy person who feels comfortable in my skin, I do beat myself up because I am influenced by societal pressure to be thin." Challenging or conforming to cultural standards of beauty both take their toll. Mindy said, "I don't think of myself as overweight. I definitely get hurt when people say mean things about my body. But it's not the most important thing in my life." She channeled that displeasure into voicing green-hued Disgust in Pixar's Oscar winning animation *Inside Out*.

In 2017, Mindy gave birth to her daughter Katherine Swati, whose middle name honored Mindy's mother. Though the baby's father remains unpublicized, her godfather is B.J. Novak. As a single mom, Mindy continued to strive. She played Mrs. Who in Disney's 2018 film adaptation of *A Wrinkle in Time*. Commenting on her co-stars Oprah Winfrey and Reese Witherspoon, Mindy said, "The acting was obviously incredible with these Oscar winners and nominees. But to learn about how they manage their companies and families — that was invaluable." Mindy also created the short-lived NBC show *Champions* and played the jewelry maker Amita in the heist movie *Ocean's 8*. She spoke at Dartmouth's graduation and bought a 5,900-square-foot Malibu beach mansion, once owned by Frank Sinatra, for $9.55 million.

Mindy founded a new television production company, Kaling International, and in 2019, created the semi-autobiographical dramedy *Late Night*. She played Molly Patel, a writer for a nighttime talk show starring Emma Thompson as the host. At Sundance, Amazon purchased the film's US distribution rights for $13 million and then contracted to publish Mindy's next book in 2020. For her fortieth birthday, Mindy donated $1,000 each to forty different charities, became one of *Elle* magazine's "Women in Hollywood," and produced Hulu's multicultural reinterpretation of the 1994 movie *Four Weddings and a Funeral*.

Next up is Mindy's Netflix comedy series *Never Have I Ever*. Inspired by Mindy's life, the character Devi is an Indian American high school sophomore, a nerd yearning for popularity. Mindy posted the role on social media and picked Toronto teen Maitreyi Ramakrishnan out of 15,000 applicants. "I wish I had a show like this growing up," said Maitreyi. "You're figuring out where you fit within your own culture, and identity is so important.... It's not only how you show yourself to the rest of the world, but also how you accept yourself."

Reese Witherspoon, who has signed up to make *Legally Blonde 3* with Mindy, concurred:

> This thing we say to kids, "You can't be it if you can't see it." Well, Mindy didn't see it growing up. She didn't see herself represented on television shows or in her favorite *SNL* or in her favorite romantic comedies or sci-fi movies. She didn't see herself in the publishing world, and she really didn't see herself on the cover of magazines. So she asked herself, "Why not me?" And she became it.

SOURCES

*Elle* [India ed.], May 2018. https://elle.in/article/mindy-kaling-cover/

*Women in the World*, 7 Apr. 2016. https://womenintheworld.com/2016/04/07/i-am-literally-living-the-dream-mindy-kaling-on-overcoming-prejudice-and-finding-success/

https://dartmouthalumnimagazine.com/articles/dialed

www.latimes.com/entertainment-arts/tv/story/2019-10-15/mindy-kaling-tv-academy-elle-women-in-hollywood

www.theguardian.com/tv-and-radio/2014/jun/01/mindy-kaling-project

# CHRISSY TEIGEN

## MODEL & ENTREPRENEUR

Born: November 30, 1985          Delta, Utah

"So many movies come out where they're putting people who have
no Asian background at all in roles, and it's frustrating because you know that there
is so much talent out there. I think it's really important to feature Asian Americans.
We're so underrepresented in every single aspect of the entertainment industry,
and I think our turn will come, and it's going to be fantastic."

Having more than 44 million social media followers is a unique 21st century accomplishment. Whatever "it" is, Chrissy Teigen has it. Wife of John Legend, the first black male Emmy-Grammy-Oscar-Tony (EGOT) award winner, and mom of kids Luna and Miles, Chrissy has worked for her multi-faceted celebrity.

"I'LL MAKE A BANANA BREAD FOR ANYONE THAT HAS ROMAINE LETTUCE. THE TRADE WILL BE MADE **6** FEET APART AND WE WILL PLACE THE GOODS ON THE FLOOR. NO FUNNY BUSINESS."

— CHRISSY TEIGEN (@CHRISSYTEIGEN), MARCH 23, 2020

Born Christine Diane Teigen (pronounced "tie-gen") in a tiny town in eastern Utah (population ~3,000), Chrissy now influences pop culture worldwide. An alluring magazine model, she has become a candid television guest, host, and producer. She broadcasts her vibrant presence in image, recipe, and tweet.

Back in the early 1980s, Chrissy's Norwegian American father Don visited Korat, Thailand and met her mother Vilailuck, a young single mom with an infant daughter Tina. The three flew to America where Chrissy was born. They lived in Idaho and had a pet pot-bellied pig named Junior. The family moved to Washington state and ran a tavern called Porky's. Her mom became known as "Pepper Thai" for her habit of eating hot food. Chrissy remembered:

> I spent my childhood in the kitchen following around Thai Mom, who pretty much made everything from scratch, using tools none of my other friends had in their homes....I remember, when my friends were over, plugging my nose and pretending to hate the exotic fish sauce my mom was using.

A cheerleader at Snohomish High School, Chrissy recalled, "Even in Seattle, you couldn't buy green papayas then. My mom kind of gave up and learned to cook corned beef and cabbage instead."

After Pepper returned to Asia to care for her ill parents, Don relocated with Chrissy to Huntington Beach, California. During her senior year, Chrissy worked at a surf shop where a photographer "discovered" her. Protective of his daughter, Don held the photographer's light reflector during her first photo shoot on the beach.

Chrissy's early modeling days dispensed tough lessons. In New York City, she applied at eleven modeling agencies. All refused her. When Chrissy signed with an agency in Miami, Florida, she lived in a "model apartment." Six girls shared two bedrooms and each paid $4,000 a month in rent.

Meanwhile, John Stephens had graduated from the University of Pennsylvania, where his roommate was a cousin of Kanye West. In 2001, John, an aspiring musician, met Kanye and then adopted the stage name of "Legend." Kanye produced John Legend's first albums, *Get Lifted* (2004) and *Once Again* (2006). John met Chrissy when she starred in one of his music videos. She had modeled for catalogs and held a briefcase of cash (along with Meghan Markle, the future British royal Duchess of Sussex) on the NBC television game show *Deal or No Deal*.

Chrissy's big break came when fellow model Brooklyn Decker introduced her to *Sports Illustrated* (*SI*) magazine. Soon Chrissy was named "Rookie of the Year" in *SI*'s 2010 swimsuit issue. Appearing in many consecutive years, she graced the cover of *SI*'s 50th anniversary issue in 2014. Though sunbathing became her claim to fame, Chrissy admitted, "I actually hate the beach. I can't swim. I hate sand. I hate water."

Considering herself lucky to have been a model, since "I am paid a good amount of money to not blink for 12 hours," Chrissy revealed that "I don't take it as seriously as a lot of the girls do." Now represented by IMG (International Management Group), she advises the next generation of aspiring girls: "Be humble. The world is really small. Word travels so fast with how you treat people. Little things go a really long way." Realizing that beautiful people can be the most insecure, Chrissy confessed that the hardest part of modeling is "when you are dieting or 'keeping it light,' people love to call you out on it.... I love food and I hate fasting."

In 2011, Chrissy started a food blog and got engaged to John. In 2013, they were invited to the White House, where John performed at President Barack Obama's inaugural ball. She cooked with Michelin-starred chef Eric Ripert on the Reserve Channel's *On the Table*. Later that year, the couple married in New York City and celebrated their wedding in Como, Italy. There, Chrissy starred in John's music video "All of Me" which became a number one song on Billboard and garnered 1.7+ billion YouTube views.

Comparing herself with her husband, Chrissy concluded,

> We are just complete polar opposites. I'm very outspoken....I open myself to everybody, all kinds of criticism...he wants to maintain this aura of mystery... with me, I almost feel it's more endearing and more fabulous if I can engage the public.

So began Chrissy's transition from supermodel to media personality. Soon she appeared on dozens of television shows, from *Entertainment Tonight* and *E!* to *Ellen*. On *The Getaway* (produced by late chef-author Anthony Bourdain), she traveled to Thailand, exploring Bangkok's floating food markets to "the art of eight limbs" (muay thai kickboxing). In 2015, she co-hosted Spike's *Lip Sync Battle* with rapper LL Cool J. Meanwhile she endorsed sunglasses, clothes, and cosmetics.

In 2016, Chrissy had a daughter Luna. Her pearl of mommy wisdom? "Having a squirmy, busy busy baby is tough." But that did not stop her from launching a bestselling cookbook *Cravings*. Chrissy said:

> I used to be embarrassed of Thai food's weird smells as a little kid (especially the strong garlic scent), but now I crave all of the different Thai spices and use endless amounts of garlic in my recipes. I've come to be proud of my heritage, instead of shying away from it.

In 2018, Chrissy had her son Miles and launched her second bestseller *Cravings: Hungry for More* in tandem with kitchenware at Target. This sequel featured a chapter of recipes from her mother, who had become a US citizen and lived with the couple in their Beverly Hills mansion.

Chrissy mixes career and motherhood, and manages with self-deprecating honesty and stamina. She showcases her kids on Instagram and Twitter, but hopes they grow up more at ease with their multiracial identity than she did. Chrissy said, "I remember feeling confused when I grew up, filling out the forms on those standardized tests. I was like, 'Am I Pacific Islander? What am I? I don't even know!' And then there was 'Other.' But I always said 'Asian' for some wild reason, even though it's a perfect 50 / 50."

Chrissy is comfortable in her own skin, portraying herself in a 2020 episode of *The Simpsons* and judging small claims cases in *Chrissy's Court* (Pepper is the bailiff) on Quibi, a streaming app for ten-minute videos. A friend of restaurateur David Chang, Chrissy accompanied him to Morocco on his 2019 Netflix series *Breakfast, Lunch & Dinner*. She founded her own TV production company (Suit and Thai) to make programs for Hulu, such as *Family Style*, a cooking talk show co-hosted by herself and Chang.

The year 2019 was a rollercoaster. *Time* magazine named Chrissy one of its "100 Most Influential People." Having made *Time's* list in 2009 and 2017, John became an eleven-time

Grammy winner, a judge on NBC's *The Voice*, and *People* magazine's "Sexiest Man Alive." Then Ron divorced Pepper, and Chrissy engaged in Twitter feuds with internet trolls. By year's end, *Vanity Fair* magazine featured Chrissy and John as "The First Family We Deserve" because of how they promote love and understanding, and challenge fear and hate.

Chrissy has shared her experiences with infertility, sadness after childbirth, and plastic surgery. In 2018, *Glamour* magazine named her one of their "Women of the Year." At that awards ceremony, her husband's introduction brought them both to tears:

> I think the world may have missed out on Chrissy's full awesomeness if it weren't for social media. She would have never fully shone the way she does if she were filtered by publicists and handlers…. Chrissy's biggest impact may be the way she proves that just by being the person you are, you can make a difference…. If you speak up about the things that you believe in, whether it's immigration rights, postpartum depression, or the joys of chicken pot pie — and if you do it authentically and without presumption, you can enlighten another human being, you can brighten people's day. What a gift that is. And what a time to do it, right now, when it's so important to amplify voices of reason, not shut them down.

SOURCES
"On the Table: Episode 7." Reserve Channel. www.youtube.com/watch?v=L9cHxxbVdvs
*Vanity Fair*, Dec. 2019.
https://stylecaster.com/chrissy-teigen-luna-racial-diversity/
www.glamour.com/story/john-legend-honors-chrissy-teigen-at-glamour-2018-women-of-the-year-awards
www.nytimes.com/2014/07/16/dining/hearty-cravings-sometimes-unfulfilled.html

# JEREMY LIN

## BASKETBALL PLAYER

Born: August 23, 1988                    Torrance, California

"... [S]ome of my mom's friends would tell her that she was wasting everyone's time by letting me play so much basketball. And so she would get criticized, but she let me play because she saw that basketball made me happy."

In 1947, Jackie Robinson broke baseball's color barrier and 5'7" Wataru Misaka became the first Asian American to play in the NBA. In 2002, the NBA's number one draft pick came from China: 7'6" Yao Ming who became "Rookie of the Year." An eight-time All-Star, Yao entered the NBA Hall of Fame with Shaquille O'Neal in 2016. The next year the Houston Rockets retired Yao's jersey #11. In 2019, Jeremy Lin was the first Asian American to become an NBA champion.

In 2010, no one predicted that 6'3" Jeremy would hold the trophy. None of the 450 players on thirty NBA teams was Asian American. Only a handful had made it in sixty years. No NBA team drafted this Harvard graduate. Less than 0.5% of NCAA Division I men's basketball players were Asian American, so no college recruited him. No one from Harvard had played in NBA since 1954.

Jeremy's college stats were noteworthy: twice Ivy League first-team and the first player with 1,450 points, 450 rebounds, 400 assists, and 200 steals. Yet his father wrote, "in high school they called my son 'Mr. Improbable.'" Palo Alto (California) coach Peter Diepenbrock liked his captain's priorities: "making plays and winning games." In 2006, Jeremy led "Paly" to a state championship and won Northern California Division II "Player of the Year" and All-State first-team honors. *San Francisco Chronicle* listed Jeremy's favorite athlete (Michael Jordan) and his dream jobs (food tester or NBA player). He owed his parents for the choices.

In 1707, Jeremy's ancestors emigrated from China's Fujian province to Taiwan. Seven generations later his father Gie-Ming graduated from the prestigious National Taiwan University. In 1977, he arrived at Old Dominion University (Norfolk, Virginia) to study Engineering and work on projects for NASA's nearby Langley Research Center. Gie-Ming met Wu Xinxin. "Shirley" came from Taiwan to learn Computer Science. The couple continued their studies at Purdue (Lafayette, Indiana), where they married.

The Lins moved to southern California, where they had Joshua (1987) and Jeremy (1988). They relocated to Palo Alto where Joseph arrived in 1992. Gie-Ming filed for bankruptcy in 1995. Bouncing back, he brought his sons to the YMCA and church to play basketball. Working at Sun Microsystems, Shirley built a National Junior Basketball program and shepherded kids onto Amateur Athletic Union teams.

At Paly, Jeremy was a small freshman who made varsity. "I was only 5-3," he said. "Luckily I grew. Maybe I was meant to be a basketball player." Gei-Ming videotaped games and Shirley was "team mom." Jeremy recalled:

> … once I got into Harvard, the same moms that were criticizing her were asking her questions about which sports their kids could play to go to Harvard. It was a funny reversal for me to see them support me in basketball, even though not many other Asian parents would have done the same.

However, college referees ignored how opponents shouted bigoted slurs at Jeremy. "The worst was at Cornell, when I was being called a c--k," Jeremy remembered. "I ended up playing terrible and getting a couple of charges and doing real out-of-character stuff." Georgetown hecklers taunted "chicken fried rice" and "beef lo mein." Yale partisans mocked him with racist stereotypes, "Hey! Can you even see the scoreboard with those eyes?"

A free agent in 2010, Jeremy auditioned in the NBA's Development Summer League. In the last game, he outplayed John Wall, the Washington Wizards' number one pick. Jeremy's parents had been laid off, so luckily his performance convinced the Golden State Warriors to sign him at the league's minimum salary. Jeremy saw little action. Before the next season, the Warriors cut him and so did the Rockets. The New York Knicks claimed him off waivers.

For weeks, Jeremy sat on the bench. Uncertain of his future, he slept at his brother Josh's or teammates' apartments. The Knicks were hobbled with injuries and defeats, leaving coach Mike D'Antoni with little left to lose. His third string point guard entered the February 4, 2012 game against New Jersey. Jeremy scored 25 points in a win. Starting the next game, he scored 28 in a second victory. Madison Square Garden went crazy.

This magical run ignited Jeremy's career. Two games later, he torched Kobe Bryant's Los Angeles Lakers for 38 points. Unaware of Jeremy before tipoff, Kobe said postgame, "If you go back and take a look, his skill level was probably there from the beginning, but no one ever noticed." Amid a host of bad media puns, one caught fire . . . "Linsanity." The NBA did not have Jeremy's jersey for sale when suddenly #17 became the hottest number in sports.

In his first five starts, Jeremy's 136 points were the most of any NBA player since 1976 (breaking Shaq's 1992 record). He was one of fifteen since 1986 who averaged 20 points, 7 assists, and 1 steal through five games. *Sports Illustrated* put Jeremy on covers in consecutive weeks (joining Jordan, Dirk Nowitzki, and Kareem Abdul-Jabbar). Then D'Antoni resigned after feuding with star forward Carmelo Anthony. In 25 starts, Jeremy averaged 18 points and 8 assists. On March 24, Jeremy hurt his left knee, which required surgery, and he never played for the Knicks again.

"I GOT TO THE POINT WHERE I WAS LIKE, 'DID I EARN IT?' I DIDN'T CONTRIBUTE THE WAY I WANTED, BUT I WAS GOOD ENOUGH TO BE ON THE TEAM AND TO BE AN **NBA** PLAYER. FOR ME, I STILL HAVE A LOT OF GOALS. I STILL HAVE A LOT OF THINGS THAT I WANT TO ACCOMPLISH. AND I STILL HAVE TIME."

—JEREMY LIN,
MAY 20, 2020

While the Rockets lured Jeremy away with a three-year, $25-million contract, *Time* named him one of the "World's Top 100 Most Influential People" and the ESPYS called him "Breakthrough Athlete of the Year."

Subject of a documentary, Jeremy started a foundation and visited Taiwan to a hero's welcome. Since Yao Ming retired, Houston promoted Jeremy with zeal. NBA Commissioner David Stern was glad to have another marketing tool in China, although he agreed that racism was why Jeremy went undrafted, "I think in the rawest sense the answer to that is yes." Regardless, the NBA scheduled a Rockets preseason game in Taiwan in October 2013. There, Jeremy remarked, "It seems like yesterday where I was holding on to my NBA career, trying to make it to the next day. For us to be in Taiwan and part of this huge extravaganza in the country where my parents grew up, it's definitely … a miracle."

In Houston, Jeremy had highlights (38 points in one 2012 game; a triple double off the bench in 2014), but was traded to the Lakers. He just missed reuniting with D'Antoni who resigned after clashing with Kobe. Earning almost $15 million but not playing on a losing team, Jeremy vented, "… it's like I'm back. At square one. Where I was before."

Incurring injuries, Jeremy passed through three more teams before joining the Toronto Raptors in 2018 for a minimal salary. Led by Kawhi Leonard, the Raptors beat the favored Warriors and became the first champs outside the United States. Jeremy played one minute in the finals, yet made history.

A few weeks later, Jeremy was despondent. No NBA team offered him a contract. At a summer press conference in Taiwan (where his brother Joseph played), he cried, "… there's a saying … 'Once you've hit rock bottom, the only way is up.' Rock bottom just seems to keep getting more and more rock bottom for me. So free agency has been tough, because I feel like in some ways the NBA's kind of given up on me."

The next month in Shanghai, Jeremy reflected, "Ironically, to be able to be OK with your weakness is one of the strongest things you could do. Who doesn't have weaknesses? We all do…. Man, try. Fail. It's OK." A few weeks later, he decided to play basketball in China where his popularity rivaled his popularity rivaled that of Kobe and the Warriors' Stephen Curry. Jeremy tweeted: "Will always cherish being able to rep Asians at the NBA level. Excited for the next step with the Beijing Ducks." Wearing his JL7 Xtep shoes, Jeremy averaged 24 points, 6 assists in his first 24 games in the Chinese Basketball Association (CBA), whose commissioner was Yao Ming. But the 2020 coronavirus caused the cancellation of sports around the globe.

On *60 Minutes* in 2013, Jeremy recalled Linsanity, "That stretch, that was the most fun that I've ever had in my life." On April 27, 2020, the MSG TV network re-aired those games for the first time for viewers under quarantine. Meanwhile Jeremy pledged up to $1 million to charity for food and medical supplies. As anti-Asian violence rose due to COVID-19 scapegoating, Jeremy wrote, "We must continue to speak up and fight racism and xenophobia in ANY form…. Each act of goodness matters. Each positive choice will add up."

The following month, Jeremy returned to China and to enthusiastic fans. The CBA prepared to resume play. He commented: "Out here, this season has been the closest thing to Linsanity in New York."

SOURCES

"Linsanity." *60 Minutes*. 7 Apr. 2013.

www.basketball-reference.com/players/l/linje01/gamelog/2012

www.espn.com/espn/feature/story/_/id/12561636/inside-jeremy-lin-life-linsanity-new-york-knicks

www.sfchronicle.com/sports/article/Jeremy-Lin-Ivy-Leaguers-called-him-racial-slurs-11139968.php

www.si.com/nba/2020/05/20/jeremy-lin-china-basketball-linsanity-redux

www.si.com/vault/2010/02/01/105899241/harvard-school-of-basketball

# BOOKS BY OUR
# AWESOME ASIAN AMERICANS

Chang, David, and Peter Meehan. *Momofuku: A Cookbook*. Clarkson Potter, 2009.

Chang, David, and Gabe Ulla. *Eat a Peach: A Memoir*, Clarkson Potter, 2020.

Inouye, Daniel K., *Journey to Washington*. Prentice-Hall, 1967.

Johnson, Dwayne, and Joseph Layden. *The Rock Says...:The Most Electrifying Man in Sports-Entertainment*. HarperEntertainment, 2000.

Kaling, Mindy. *Is Everyone Hanging Out Without Me? (And Other Concerns)*. Crown Archetype, 2011.

---. *Why Not Me?* Crown Archetype, 2015.

Kochiyama, Yuri. *Passing It On – A Memoir*. UCLA Asian American Studies Center Press, 2004.

Lee, Bruce. *Chinese Gung Fu: The Philosophical Art of Self-Defense*. Black Belt Communications, 1987.

---. *Tao of Jeet Kune Do*. Black Belt Communications, 1975.

Lee, Sammy. *Diving*. Atheneum, 1979.

Nadella, Satya. *Hit Refresh*. HarperBusiness, 2017.

Osato, Sono. *Distant Dances*. Knopf, 1980.

Teigen, Chrissy. *Cravings: Recipes for All the Food You Want to Eat*. Clarkson Potter Publishers, 2016.

---. *Cravings: Hungry for More*. Clarkson Potter Publishers, 2018.

Zia, Helen. *Asian American Dreams: The Emergence of an American People*. Farrar, Straus and Giroux, 2000.

---, and Susan B. Gall, eds. *Notable Asian Americans*. Gale, 1994.

# Acknowledgments

Always to Hana, first and foremost. To the Kirk Madge Reunion including Microphone Lad and Captain Yesterday, and to my very cool collaborators Oliver and Juan. Thanks to Esposito's Bakery, Santarpio's Pizza, and Roy's Coldcuts for keeping me fed. Thanks to Kicking Horse Coffee for keeping me awake. Thanks to the bands Big Thief, Land of Talk, Hopalong, Widow's Peak, Snail Mail, Middle Kids, and the Houselights for great sounds while I work. Thanks to my unicycle for giving me, what else, balance.

– Phil Amara

- - -

I am indebted to my parents, siblings, and family. Plus, I am grateful for the help of Professor Lorraine Dong, who edited with thorough and invaluable advice. I appreciate the support of Lorraine and her SFSU colleague Jeannie Woo who share the study of Asian American children's literature with the next generation of college students and educators.

Thanks to Kay Fong, Tai-Ling Wong, Kim Wong, Helen Zia, Dolly Gee, and Jane Luu for reviewing their respective biographies — your feedback was most welcome. Kudos to Phil and Juan whose countless creative contributions enriched the process and results.

– Oliver Chin

- - -

As an artist, I have been influenced in my career by the visual media, mostly by what I saw on the big screen in my youth. Many Asian American actors and actresses have been a great point of reference for my storytelling, not only by their performances, but also by their whole careers and lives. James Hong, Mako Iwamatsu, George Takei, Cary-Hiroyuki Tagawa, Noriyuki "Pat" Morita, Margaret Cho, John Cho, Lucy Liu, Joan Chen, Grace Park, Daniel Dae Kim, Steven Yeun, Daniel Pudi, Ken Jeong, and Ming-Na Wen, among many other performers, have been present in the stories that have fed my creativity all these years, making this global culture we share even more rich. And now I get to enjoy all the characters they bring to life with my son.

And finally, I would like to thank Oliver Chin, the Asian American writer who believed in my work and allowed me to pay a little homage to all the personalities presented in this book.

– Juan Calle